OPPORTUNITIES

in

S0-AHJ-167

Commercial Art and Graphic Design Careers

REVISED EDITION

BARBARA GORDON

VGM Career Books

Chicago   New York   San Francisco   Lisbon   London   Madrid   Mexico City
Milan   New Delhi   San Juan   Seoul   Singapore   Sydney   Toronto

Library of Congress Cataloging-in-Publication Data

Gordon, Barbara.
    Opportunities in commercial art and graphic design careers / Barbara
Gordon. — Rev. ed.
        p.   cm. — (VGM opportunities series)
      ISBN 0-07-141149-6
      1. Commercial art—United States—Marketing.   2. Graphic arts—United
States—Marketing.   I. Title.   II. Series.

  NC1001.6G68   2003
  741.6′068′8—dc21   2003050090

  2 3 4 5 6 7 8 9 0   LBM/LBM   2 1 0 9 8 7 6 5 4

ISBN 0-07-141149-6

Interior design by Rattray Design

McGraw-Hill books are available at special quantity discounts to use as premiums and sales promotions, or for use in corporate training programs. For more information, please write to the Director of Special Sales, Professional Publishing, McGraw-Hill, Two Penn Plaza, New York, NY 10121-2298. Or contact your local bookstore.

This book is printed on acid-free paper.

CONTENTS

Foreword   vii

1. Choosing a Career   1

Definitions. Do you have talent? Selecting an art
school. Night school. Internships. Freelance or salaried
employee? Galleries and agents. Private commissions.
Commercial illustrators. Web designers. Art directors.
Designers.

2. Freelance Commercial Illustrators   17

Major markets. Artistic style. Assembling a selling
portfolio.

3. Art Directors   25

Qualifications. Working in an advertising agency.
Print art direction. Television art direction. Types of

advertising agencies. Locations of advertising agencies. Art director training programs. Finding a job as an art director.

4. **More Opportunities in Advertising Agencies and Other Companies**   **41**

Collateral departments. Art buyers. Comp artists. Storyboard artists. Layout and pasteup artists. Assistant art directors. Freelance art direction.

5. **Graphic Design Opportunities**   **47**

Graphic design specialties. Design studio. Art studio. Animation studio.

6. **Book Publishing Market**   **55**

Trade books. Educational publishers. Paperback books. Freelance work. Book packagers. Specialized publishers.

7. **Editorial Design: Magazines and Newspapers**   **61**

Magazine publishing. Newspaper design.

8. **Television and Film Markets**   **71**

Local television. Network television. Cable television. Film industry.

9. **Corporate Art Departments and Promotion Departments**   77

Responsibilities of corporate advertising and sales promotion departments. Sales support. Institutional advertising. Corporate advertising department staff. Newcomer advantages.

10. **Other Special Career Opportunities**   87

Architectural and interior design firms. Retail design firms. Greeting card companies. Specialty cards. Printers. Agents. Fashion market.

11. **Are You Ready for the Real World?**   95

Portfolios. Job searches. Fine artist versus reality. What about art direction? Where do you fit in?

Appendix A: Professional Societies and
   Organizations   103
Appendix B: Periodicals   109
Appendix C: Training Programs/Schools   113
Bibliography   165

Foreword

DURING THE GULF War, media such as television and the press were used for the first time as strategic tools. More than ever before, media are influencing the extent to which politicians, celebrities, and others alike are being lifted up to great heights or dashed to the ground as the result of fast and believable graphic communications.

Commercial art and graphic design are touching all our lives in highly influential and complex ways that would have been considered incredible just a short time ago. Consider the recent movie *Independence Day*, with its seamless digital sequences: as I am sure you know, the scene in which the White House blew up was a computer implementation of a graphic design—a bunch of numbers. Nonetheless, it looked very real.

Expect some games that incorporate virtual reality technology to become as commonplace as video games in shopping malls within the next few years. Expect at least one major scandal involving the manipulation of digital images, changing photographic evidence, during this period of time.

The information age is truly with us. The Internet has made design more accessible and has provided the means for printed media to rival television's speed, graphic persuasiveness, and quality.

In spite of this, the role of the graphic designer is becoming more complex. There is more information to assimilate more quickly, more technology to understand and master, more competition, more creative possibility, more flexibility, and more freedom.

All of this new technology, however, has created the need for new ethics and a new view of moral issues. For example, it is not ethical to copy the work of others; you may not take a photograph and change it digitally without the permission of the photographer, nor may you then call it your own. It is also unethical to copy a computer program or a typeface to avoid paying for it.

If you decide to pursue a career in commercial art, you will need to deal with these issues. You will have to compete, but you will have the same tools as the others, and so you can win. You will be a part of a fast-moving and evolving field that fundamentally influences all other environments.

A good graphic designer can transcend the technology, not be intimidated by it, and use this rich array of new tools to produce graphic materials that make all our lives better.

This is your challenge. We all need you, and if you get involved, you can make a difference.

Mark Batty
President and CEO
International Typeface Corporation

1

Choosing a Career

Most readers of this book probably have at least two things in common: the desire to be an artist and the desire to make a living at it. The level of resemblance between one reader and another will drop dramatically at this point, since there are many kinds of artists and many ways to make a living with art.

Definitions

At this point, it will be helpful to define some of the different terms and job titles that are used in the art world. Here are some of the more common ones:

Fine Artists

The fine artist is the person who comes closest to producing works of "art for art's sake." He or she may be a painter, sculptor, graphic artist, or specialist in several art media. The fine artist is not a commercial artist, although he or she may sell works of art and often makes a handsome living at it. If the fine artist devotes major time to art or makes most of a living at selling his or her work, that artist can be designated a professional artist.

There are several ways that the fine artist might sell work. The professional fine artist may do work on commission. A government official, a religious group, or other institutions or individuals might order or commission a work of art, such as a mural, a portrait, or a sculpture. The artist, or the artist's agent, will make an agreement as to the basic nature of the work, when it is to be completed, and how and when the artist will be paid. This is, of course, a business transaction, but it does not make the artist a commercial artist. Even under a commission, the fine artist will be expected to have quite a bit of freedom in carrying out the work of art according to his or her own concept, style, and technique. Fine artists do not usually get commissions until their work is fairly well known and their professional reputations are established. Even so, commissions do not come along very regularly, and fine artists must usually be prepared to support their work and themselves in between sales and commissions. The professional fine artist may also get income through gallery sales, sales by an art agent, support from foundations or grants, teaching, and prizes and awards.

Commercial Artists

Commercial artists, however, are in business to sell art products that other people need and want to buy. Within this category are many different kinds of artists—book illustrators, package designers, art directors, photographers, keyline/pasteup artists, medical illustrators, technical illustrators, fashion designers, cartoonists, furniture and textile designers, children's book illustrators, and so forth.

The commercial artist earns income usually in one of two ways: from working for an hourly wage or a salary on the staff of various kinds of companies (design, advertising, public relations, book or magazine publishers, and so forth), or from working as a freelance artist who agrees to do one job at a time for a company, often under a contract.

The commercial artist on the staff of an organization is a paid employee; the freelance artist is self-employed. The staff artist gets a regular paycheck for the work he or she does; the freelance artist does one project, gives the client a bill or invoice, and gets paid for that one job.

The freelance artist must spend a substantial amount of time rounding up new jobs, keeping accounts for tax records, and paying for his or her own medical insurance. To be a freelance artist, one must be prepared to run an art career like a business.

There are many similarities between the fine artist's career and the freelance commercial artist's career. The basic difference is that the fine artist's work is the development of that person's unique talent to its fullest potential in a life's work of expression of the artist's concepts; the commercial artist's work always contributes to the advancement of other people's ideas, products, and businesses. The commercial artist's work can and should also have artistic integrity within that commercial role.

For many artists, the deepest satisfaction comes from work in fine art. Many commercial artists also work in fine art, on their own time, and many produce very good work. Some of them also supplement their commercial art income by occasional sales of fine art pieces. And fine artists often do commercial artwork. For example, a painter of outstanding fine art may do the illustrations for a book or a series of posters. So, the line between fine artists and commercial artists is not always sharply defined. It is an important distinction, however, and it does have significant meaning. Consequently, you'll want to think seriously about your career and choosing the schools where you will study.

Graphic Designers

The graphic designer is a commercial artist who designs, or oversees others who design, a multitude of products used in modern life. Think about it. A graphic designer has designed the artistic elements of our newspapers, books, and magazines; the advertisements in our media; the labels and other visual elements of all the boxes, cans, and bottles in our supermarkets and hardware stores; the huge billboards along our highways; the company logos that appear on the sides of trucks and trains; and the websites that we read and research everyday. Thousands of graphic designers work in almost every business in our economy. As our society moves from an "industrial economy" to an "information economy," jobs in graphic design are expected to increase steadily.

Perhaps you want to be a fine artist whose works will hang in galleries and museums; an award-winning art director working in a major New York agency; a designer whose graphics enliven annual reports; or a television producer creating documentaries, specials, or local station news. Regardless of what part of the art world you want to play a role in, you must start with basic art education, and choosing the right art school can be one of the most critical decisions that you make concerning your ultimate art career.

Do You Have Talent?

Obviously, it is fundamentally important for a person considering a career in art to examine critically her or his talent—that innate ability to draw, paint, and compose art. If you were the high school student who always amused your classmates by drawing caricatures or doing beautiful renderings freehand, or if your aptitude tests have consistently shown a high degree of talent in the field of art, a career as a painter or illustrator might be for you. But remember: painting techniques—the technical aspect of an art career—can be taught in any art school, but talent is innate and is not teachable. Professional advice should be sought to determine whether you have the talent necessary to make a living in the painting area. There are many people who can draw and paint adequately enough to become art directors or designers, but they cannot and should not rely on their art talent (or lack of it) to make a living.

Get plenty of advice from teachers, professional artists, and agents. Be realistic in your candid appraisal of your own art talent before making any art education or career decision. Remember that talent is an important part of becoming an artist, but you must also have the skill. Unlike a few years ago, almost all of graphic design today is done on the computer. Designers looking for top jobs must have the essential computer skills and know the basic design software programs such as Illustrator, Photoshop, and QuarkXpress to be considered for a job. These programs are taught in art school, or you can take special classes and read tutorial books to learn them on your own.

An excellent online directory, petersons.com, lists schools, specializations, size of departments, and other important information that will be of value to a student contemplating a career in art. In making your final determination, you should follow the procedures outlined in the next section of this chapter, "Selecting an Art School," keeping in mind your ultimate objective as a career choice. Also refer to Appendix C for a complete list of training programs and art schools in the United States.

Selecting an Art School

When choosing an art school, you should determine the strengths and weaknesses of each school as they relate to your own personal interests in art. For example, if you are interested in becoming an art director in an advertising agency, in publishing, or in another type of business, you should consider those art schools that are strongly oriented to the areas of advertising and editorial design and illustration. This means the emphasis of the curriculum will be geared more to the commercial aspects of art than the aesthetic areas.

On the other hand, if you are interested in becoming a fine arts painter and want your paintings to hang in galleries or be sold to private collections, then you should go to a school that emphasizes painting in the classical tradition and also places emphasis on art theory, aesthetics, and history.

A fine arts background will prepare you for a career as a painter, but you will also want to take some basic business courses if you expect to be in business for yourself. Bookkeeping and accounting, business law, and business correspondence will all be useful.

If your main interests are in the area of art education, teaching art and art history, then colleges that place an emphasis on art history and art teaching techniques would be much more appropriate for you than commercial or fine arts–oriented art schools.

If you are interested in becoming a commercial illustrator, you will want to investigate those schools that concentrate on the commercial art field. The faculties of these schools, for example, may include working commercial illustrators and photographers who are dealing on a daily basis with the joys and frustrations of producing illustrations and photographs for advertisements in a variety of media. They will prepare you for a career in commercial arts, through both subject matter and techniques that are very different from the education you would need for fine arts painting or sculpture. There are some schools that offer internships that will provide hands-on experience while you learn the business.

Consequently, before embarking on a college or commercial art program, carefully investigate each school not only by reading the various catalogs and department and school literature, but also by visiting the schools and observing classes. Talk to graduates and students attending the school so that you can determine in your own mind where the school places its emphasis. You may also want to contact friends or family members in specific art fields who can offer valuable advice.

Night School

For many students who are unable to afford education on a full-time basis, night school can be a means of getting a good art education while working during the day in a variety of studios or agencies and gaining practical art experience. Many a successful artist has earned his or her "artist living" by working at a job by day and studying art at night. This is becoming an economic necessity and a way of life for the aspiring artist, much more than it was in earlier times.

Students also can take private lessons with either commercial illustrators or fine art painters to learn how to paint and apply this skill to the commercial art or fine arts fields.

A word of caution: although it is technically possible to make a transition between fine art and commercial art, often it is much more difficult psychologically to "shift gears" from one field to the other. Consequently, you should look at both areas—the commercial art field and the fine arts field—and decide on which feels most comfortable and practical to you regardless of the financial considerations. Be true to yourself, because in the end, the only person you will have to please is yourself.

Internships

Some universities and colleges offer internship programs that a potential graphic artist may want to investigate. An internship is an unpaid position at an advertising agency, gallery, museum, or publishing company, or at a corporation or bank with an art investment program. These internship programs allow students to get invaluable on-the-job experience in the fields of their choice or to gain exposure to a wide variety of possible career areas in the arts and graphics fields.

Interns may work nights or weekends so that the internships do not interfere with classes. An intern may work on a wide variety of projects at the institution involved and may do anything from research to cataloging works of art. Internships give the potential artist the opportunity to get hands-on experience in a field he or she might consider entering. Additionally, internships sometimes lead to paying jobs.

To get information on internships, students should start by calling and researching websites of local art schools, colleges, and universities, as well as the career centers at their local high schools. For example, a student in the New York area might contact New York University, Adelphi University, Columbia University, or the Fashion Institute of Technology, as well as his or her high school career guidance department.

Freelance or Salaried Employee?

Another career choice you will have to make at some point in your life—a career decision that is on a par with the kind of art education you choose to pursue—is the decision as to whether you want to be a freelancer or a salaried employee. The difference is important in both psychological and economic terms.

What Is a Freelancer?

A freelancer is someone who works for himself or herself, accepting assignments from other sources and performing those services for a per-hour rate or set fee. The freelancer is on no one's payroll, receives no benefits from any company, and is ultimately responsible for his or her own actions. The freelance artist is an independent businessperson/artist accountable only to himself or herself and to the clients for whom art services are performed.

Obviously, the advantage of being a freelancer is that everything you do is directly traceable to you (both good and bad), and any money you make is your money and does not have to be split with anyone else except the IRS. Being a freelancer means that you can build your own personal reputation in the art field, and the greater the reputation you achieve as an artist, painter, or designer, the higher the prices you can charge. On the other side of the coin, you work your own hours and must maintain great self-discipline and organization. You control your own destiny—you are your own boss.

The primary disadvantage of being a freelancer is the problem of guaranteeing steady work. If you are just starting out, it may be difficult to find work because you do not yet have a reputation in the field. Freelancers must perform the difficult dual job of selling themselves and their work constantly as well as actually doing the work. Consequently, there are often working cycles of highs and lows. In other words, a freelancer may have long dry spells where there is no work in the art studio. It takes a certain type of personality to deal with this kind of situation. However, the potential for making tremendous amounts of money is there for the successful freelancer—an opportunity not so readily available when one works for a company.

What Is a Salaried Employee?

The salaried employee is the direct opposite of the freelancer. The salaried employee is directly responsible to the company for whom he or she works and performs design or art services under the direction of supervisors. The salaried employee is not a free agent. Salaried employees work within the structure of a company or organization and do not have the freedom or flexibility to perform many of the things they would like to do for their own satisfaction. However, salaried employees are guaranteed an income for as long as they hold that job. For many people, the security and safety of a salary, as well as health insurance and other valuable benefits, far outweigh the freedom of opportunity of the freelancer.

Whether you become a salaried artist or an art director or designer with a company, advertising agency, or studio; or whether you become a freelance artist, illustrator, or designer depends a great deal upon the kind of person you are:

- Do you like the solitude of working alone?
- Do you revel in the challenge of seeking work in the open marketplace, of being a "salesperson" for your work?

- Do you like to control your own work pace—for example, working for seven days straight and then doing nothing for two?
- Can you accept the fluctuation of your income as "the way the business is," always feeling that you can and will meet your responsibilities?
- Do you enjoy taking risks?

These are all characteristics of the freelance life. If the thought of dealing with any of these things causes you stress or worry, then the life of a salaried employee may be a better choice.

It cannot be overemphasized that the critical thing about any career choice is choosing a career that you enjoy, that you are good at, and that gives you true financial security and psychological happiness. Too many people lead lives of quiet desperation because they have not taken the time to realistically examine themselves and what makes them happy before making their career choices.

Galleries and Agents

Most art done by a fine arts painter is sold through art galleries. A gallery is simply a structure specifically set up to display works of art by a variety of artists and to sell these works of art to the interested public. Galleries earn their income by taking a percentage of the retail sales price of any fine arts painting. This "cut" by the gallery covers its cost of rent, electricity, special opening parties, and promotion, as well as profit. However, it is important to remember that although the gallery sets a price for each and every painting displayed, the real price is the one that is actually paid when a painting is sold. Anyone can put any price on any painting, but if the price is ludicrously high, it will not sell. The gallery, because of its knowledge of the fine arts field, will usually price a painting very competitively so as to move the painting more quickly than a private artist would, who has no knowledge of the prices currently being charged in the fine arts field. In essence, the gallery becomes the selling agent for the fine artist.

The art business is highly competitive, and it is extremely difficult for any artist to become accepted by a gallery. However, this condition should not prevent the individual artist from trying to get a gallery connection. In fact, the artist should be more persistent than ever because of the competition.

Galleries can range from the very prestigious galleries found on Madison Avenue in New York to small, local, but perhaps also elite galleries in many of the small towns across the country. The fine arts painters should investigate very carefully as many galleries as possible, observing the style of art each gallery displays to make sure that the gallery is compatible with the kind of art the fine artist is painting. In addition, the fine arts painter should observe the prices being charged by the gallery. Are they compatible with what the artist believes his or her paintings are worth? How aggressively does the gallery promote each artist, and through what means? Direct mail? Opening parties? Press releases? All of this has an effect on how much exposure the fine artist will get to the public. In other words, the painter must feel comfortable with the gallery chosen, for the painter is literally entrusting his or her economic life as an artist to that gallery.

Private Commissions

Other sources of income that we have mentioned previously for fine arts painters are private commissions. These commissions may range from portraits of the neighbor's children to special subject paintings for corporate collections. Fine arts painters have also found careers as decorative painters. Decorative painters are hired by companies to paint murals in restaurants or offices, or by individuals to paint specific designs or murals in their homes.

The development of a good, lucrative market for a fine arts painter can take considerably longer and be somewhat more difficult than the road taken by a commercial illustrator. However, if the fine arts painter believes strongly in the individual aspects of his or her painting, then choosing this road may make the most sense.

Commercial Illustrators

The commercial illustrator is also a freelancer, but he or she performs art services for specific commercial clients. For example, an advertising agency or a company may want a particular product or people situation illustrated for a national advertisement. A commercial illustrator would be called in to perform this function. The commercial illustrator would be working under specific direction from the art director and client and would not have the degree of personal freedom inherent in the work of the fine artist. Fees would be paid in relation to the complexity of the job, the reputation of the artist, where the particular illustration will be used, how many times the image will be used, and the client's budget. The essential point to remember for any person considering a commercial illustrator's career is that the commercial illustrator, although technically a freelancer and in business for himself or herself, must take direction from those people who are paying the bill, and so the artistic freedom may be restricted.

Specific job opportunities and career opportunities for the freelance commercial illustrator will be examined in detail later in this book. For now, all that is important is to remember the difference between the fine arts painter and the commercial illustrator, both of whom may be excellent painters but have taken an entirely different approach toward the career that will bring them the most personal satisfaction. The "ideal" career for an artist may be that of being a successful commercial illustrator and also selling art through galleries. This artist has the best of both worlds.

Web Designers

The Web designer is a specialized graphic designer who creates Web pages for the Internet, making information and design available at our fingertips. Almost every company, school, restaurant, and organization has a website, making Web designers very high in demand. It is commonplace now for most companies to hire a full-time Web designer. Web designers will use both HTML language and special software to create Web pages. They will also need to know basic computer skills and programs and have a sense for color and typography. Knowing Web design is a powerful tool for a designer to have in today's design environment. The beginning Web designer will usually start out with a higher salary than the graphic designer. Web designers are also frequently hired on a freelance basis, and they can often make a great deal of money doing so.

Art Directors

The art director, who may or may not be an artist or photographer, has the main function of directing the creation of advertisements, magazine formats, book layouts, or annual reports. An art director may utilize both illustration and photography in his or her work.

The concepts and responsibilities of the art director's job will be explained later, but for now, it is enough to know that the art director is the person who buys both illustration and photography for particular projects and is responsible for procuring services, artists, and photographers on a "need-to-hire" basis.

The art director must know design, type, and printing processes; have computer skills to solve the art and design problems of the job; and have several years of experience. Art directors, for the most part, are employees of an advertising agency, book or magazine publisher, or other company, but they can also be hired on a freelance basis.

Designers

The designer may or may not be a freelancer. There are many excellent designers currently employed either by design firms or by other companies. Many other designers operate their own firms, turning out award-winning designs for corporate clients, packaging firms, and other customers. Any commercial artist, whether an art director, a painter, an illustrator, or a filmmaker, must have a good sense of design, since solving the design problem for the client is part of the business of art. However, designers frequently work in planning, conceptualizing, and administrating, and rarely will they do any painting on a project on their own. They are responsible for designing and managing a project—a display, brochure, or annual report—from start to finish.

Many opportunities exist today to be a fine arts painter, a commercial artist, an art director, or a designer. This book will outline for you the advantages and disadvantages of each profession as well as many other "satellite" careers available to the person interested in art. Remember: nothing is forever, and it is quite possible that decisions made today may lead to different decisions ten, twenty, or even thirty years from now. But you must make some kind of decision to begin, and go in some direction now, and it is hoped that this book will serve as a guide for you to consider your own future in the art field.

Whether you go into fine art or commercial art, or into design or television, you should always be aware of the fact that commercial and professional art is a business and that consequently the professional painter, commercial illustrator, photographer, or graphic designer must treat it as such. Talent plus opportunity plus diligence is the key equation for success in the art field, and there are no shortcuts to reach it. You must evaluate your talent, acquire the necessary knowledge and education to improve that talent, and commit yourself to whatever aspect of the art field interests you. It is not of such great consequence whether you paint as a fine artist for your own free spirit or as a commercial artist for the money, as it is that you must be true to your own personal goals and commit yourself to the fulfillment of those goals.

2

FREELANCE COMMERCIAL
ILLUSTRATORS

WERE YOU ONE of the students in your classes who doodled on your papers, fantasizing about becoming an illustrator? Did you wish you could create the kind of art that you love to do for exorbitantly high prices? That fantasy could come true!

However, when considering a career as a freelance artist, prospective commercial artists must take many realistic elements into consideration.

The freelance artist has the freedom of being an independent contractor, as well as the responsibility that goes with being in business for himself or herself. It must be remembered that as a freelance artist you *are* in business for yourself. This means that you are responsible for obtaining studio space and taking care of all overhead costs such as telephone, rent, and supplies. It means being responsible for the cost of promoting yourself to the art field; for the collection and payment of federal, state, and local taxes; and for the many other responsibilities that are part of being in business for yourself. This also includes health insurance and any licenses you may need to establish your business. Therefore, it is vitally important for any persons considering careers as freelance artists to consider whether they have the temperament and the psychological toughness to exist without the security of a weekly paycheck and the benefits provided by most employers.

Some freelance artists have found that the stress involved in running their own businesses and creating finished works of art at the same time is too great a burden. Consequently, many move back into the corporate or studio staff area, where they do not have to worry about the responsibilities associated with being an independent businessperson.

Major Markets

Freelance artists must always be concerned about the markets for their art. Some of the major markets are:

1. **Advertising**. This includes many of the advertising agencies in the country as well as corporate and public relations advertising departments. It should be noted that the majority of artwork that is done for advertising clients is often "hard sell" in nature, since the primary purpose of an advertisement is to sell the product manufactured by a client. It is important for freelance artists to understand that their art will be heavily art-directed by agencies, clients, and other personnel, and that often freedom of expression may not be a factor in the assignment.

2. **Magazine and editorial**. These are markets where freelance artists can often do more freely creative work than in the advertising area. Often, the artist in the magazine and editorial fields is

called upon to illustrate areas of a magazine where photography either will not be used or is not appropriate. Generally, deadlines are not as tight as those found in the advertising market, and artists have more artistic maneuverability, which could mean more creative satisfaction.

3. **Book publishing**. Many freelance artists make an excellent living working in publishing, a field that includes several major categories:

- The trade book field, in which hardcover and paperback books are sold through company-owned or independent bookstores
- The mass-market field, in which paperback books are usually sold through bookstores, variety stores, drugstores, supermarkets, and the like
- The textbook field—along with various other reference and special-interest fields— in which books are sold primarily to school and reference-materials markets

In general, the artist is able to do artwork under comfortable deadlines and often has the opportunity to create expressive artwork for use on the outside or inside of the books. Because they are often unable to handle the workload, book publishers hire freelance designers frequently to design book covers and interiors. Financially, the book publishing area is not generally a high-paying one, but freelancing for publishing houses can be lucrative. It is often possible to build relationships with particular publishing houses and do projects for them on an ongoing basis.

4. **Corporate/industrial**. Many artists provide artwork for annual reports, stockholder brochures, sales brochures, websites, and many other associated needs for the corporate/industrial mar-

ket. Artwork can be produced through advertising agencies specializing in the corporate and industrial worlds, or it can be produced directly for the corporation. In some firms, it is also possible for a freelance artist to be hired on a temporary basis.

5. **Recording companies**. This field provides a large market for artwork and photography for use on CD cases and for the distribution needs of the music stores. Most record companies are in New York or Los Angeles. One big advantage of working for recording companies is the tremendous freedom given to the artist to create and execute concepts on the behalf of musical groups or individuals who seek out and appreciate unusual and exciting art and design.

6. **Newspapers**. The newspaper represents a tremendous opportunity for an illustrator, since newspapers still have great demands for black-and-white artwork. Most artwork is black and white because of the cost limitations of newspaper production. Whether the artist works for the newspaper as a staff artist or as an independent freelancer, the artist can often make a reasonable living in this area.

7. **Design firms**. Design firms specialize in a tremendous amount of corporate communications, including annual reports, sales brochures, displays, websites, and so forth. These firms represent a sizable market for the freelance artist. Some firms may also hire a graphic designer temporarily when workloads are high.

There are many other areas that utilize freelance artwork, and ferreting out these markets is one of the challenges to the freelance artist.

Freelance designers need to be concerned about promoting themselves to the many markets that might use their work. This promotion can be done through regular direct mail, E-mail, phone calls, advertising, listings in directories, special shows, and other forms. Some artists will choose to create their own unique promotional piece to leave with a prospective client, as well as creating a website and online portfolio that clients may easily access. Promotion is the most important part of the freelance scene, and the freelance artist must develop a strong and effective promotion program to reach potential customers.

Graphic designers must also be concerned about pricing their work in these various markets. Pricing can be one of the most difficult areas of freelancing, and yet ultimately it represents the bottom line for anyone making a career in art. There are excellent sources available on the market, including *Graphic Artists Guild Handbook: Pricing & Ethical Guidelines*, to help freelancers effectively price their jobs. A good sense for pricing will come primarily through working in the field and through experience acquired by pricing various jobs on a weekly basis.

In addition to all of the practical aspects previously outlined, there are two other major factors that are critical to success in the freelance art area. These are the development of artistic style and the production of a professional-quality portfolio.

Artistic Style

There are many markets out there that utilize certain artistic styles. An artist does not necessarily need to have a specific style or "look" to break into a certain market, but in some cases, it does help. For instance, some illustrators may be hired because the style of their illustrations fits with the client's needs. Nowadays, with technology so easily accessible and the growing number of talented designers, clients are looking for creative individuals who will bring something fresh to their projects.

In many market areas, the artist has more flexibility as far as style is concerned. However, the freelance artist must be aware of what he or she is selling in these markets and, without sacrificing personal artistic freedom, should gear the style of the work to those areas. It is important to note that the freelance artist in the commercial field is in the business of selling a product. He or she should be well aware of what styles are "hot"—current, fashionable, and saleable—in specific market areas so as to take advantage of the trends. Naturally, artists as creative people are also individuals, and it is important for the artist to be content and happy with the kinds of artistic styles developed for particular markets. Perhaps a designer will choose not to compete in a certain style, even though it may mean less work in particular market areas, or possibly less money than the competition. These are personal decisions that must be made by each freelance artist, but the area of style is perhaps the most important facet of determining the kind of freelance artist one becomes.

Assembling a Selling Portfolio

The other key item for any freelance artist in a commercial field is the development of the selling portfolio. Once an artist has determined the style in which to work, then a professional portfolio, containing the right subject matter for use in various markets, must be drawn together. The portfolio ultimately becomes the main selling tool of the freelance artist.

Some good sources of information for the freelance artist who is compiling a portfolio include the annual *RSVP: The Directory of Illustration and Design* and the *2003 Artist's & Graphic Designer's*

Market: 2,100+ Places to Sell Your Illustrations, Fine Art, Graphic Designs and Cartoons by Mary Cox. These books will show the freelance artist the kind of artwork being purchased in the marketplace, so that the artist will recognize not only the competition but also the kind and variety of art styles being bought. In addition, it is important for the potential freelance artist to attend seminars, workshops, and programs that emphasize commercial aspects as compared to fine arts areas. These are often offered through art schools.

The freelance artist is faced every day with new and exciting and different challenges. Usually a successful freelance artist can make a good living, but although financial potential exists for the freelance designer, nothing is guaranteed as far as income or reputation. There are thousands of new commercial artists entering the freelance field every year who are competing with each other and with older and more established artists. It is a constant battle not only to expand markets for artwork but also to preserve one's existing markets.

One of the best ways to learn about the freelance field is to talk to artists who are currently working in it. This will help you to get a realistic view of the opportunities available, as well as provide a forum for a candid discussion of some of the problems. For artists who truly like being in business for themselves and who truly enjoy the freedom to solve artistic problems on their own and get paid for it, being a freelance artist in today's competitive market can be a challenging and very exciting opportunity.

3

ART DIRECTORS

AN ART DIRECTOR—whether a member of an advertising agency, a corporation, a magazine, a book publishing company, or some other organization—is responsible for buying artwork and photography and incorporating that artwork and photography into an overall design concept—be it an advertisement, a direct mail piece, a movie poster, or some other piece of commercial art. The job title of "art director" literally says what the function of this position is—to direct the development and production of some form of art in print or film media. It stands to reason, then, that the two prime requisites of being a good art director are being able to create ideas and being able to manage people.

Qualifications

The art director has an art and design background, usually accompanied by several years of experience. He or she should be able to develop a series of ideas and concepts that will increase the effectiveness of the campaign to sell a client's products. Remember: the art director is primarily concerned with translating the major selling points of a client's product into a visual presentation. The art director, in essence, is a salesperson using images instead of words, but all advertising is always geared to selling a product and not just creating a "pretty picture."

The personal qualities of the ideal art director should include:

• **Some drawing ability**. It is not necessary for the art director to be a highly accomplished artist, because professional artists can be hired to carry out the art director's plans. But the art director must know how to draw reasonably well, because he or she will need to put down many concepts on paper in an acceptable fashion.

• **A way with words**. Much time will also be spent in dialogue with the copywriter, the account executive, and other key personnel concerning the overall advertising strategy. Consequently, although the art director eventually will translate the ideas into pictures, he or she should be able to convey, through words, the necessary concepts and ideas so that people will understand the goal for each project. An art director must also be able to give clear instructions to direct others.

• **Excellent presentation skills**. The higher the position in any advertising agency, publishing company, or corporation, the more the art director will be called upon to present ideas to clients. A skillful speaker is a definite plus for the advertising agency. A great campaign may fail to catch the eye of a client because the art director was unable to translate the visual ideas into a dynamic presentation. The art director should be able to effectively present ideas both visually and verbally to clients, as well as manage the personnel of the advertising agency, public relations firm, or other employer.

• **A strong philosophy about budgets**. Much of the art director's work will be estimating and controlling the costs of projects, perhaps in both print advertising and television commercials. Although it is not necessary that the art director be a mathematician, he or she should have an appreciation for the client's budget and should be able to effectively control costs as the projects are developed.

• **A knowledge of both illustration and photography**. One of the art director's major functions will be to evaluate portfolios submitted by commercial illustrators and photographers. The skill to evaluate portfolios will come with experience, but the art director should be well versed and aware of what is new in the field, who the hot talent is, and what styles will be effective. This knowledge will help him or her to make an intelligent decision when it comes time to choose an illustrator or photographer to work on important projects.

• **A cooperative and personable relationship with employers, fellow employees, clients, and freelance artists**. The effective art director is a professional who has a full appreciation of the business aspects of his or her art and can maintain a cordial, professional, and productive attitude toward all members on the project team.

• **A working knowledge of both television and print production**. This includes knowing how the printing process works, how to color-correct proofs of print material, and how to evaluate the many facets of television production. It is not necessary for the art director to know completely every single facet of television and print production, but he or she should have a working knowledge of the technology and its uses.

Working in an Advertising Agency

To understand an art director's role more clearly, let us first examine how an art director functions in an advertising agency, by far the largest employer of art directors. An advertising agency is an agency that produces a variety of advertisements—magazines and newspaper ads, television and radio commercials, billboards, and other ads—for clients. An agency is an independent contractor that works for a variety of clients in a variety of industries, and it is compensated either by a set fee or by a percentage commission of all media costs (television, magazines, and so forth). One of the costs involved in the production and placement of an advertisement is the cost of the art director's time and talent.

In advertising, all of the art director's work begins and ends with the needs of a client's account. If there are no accounts, there is no work; but as soon as an account has been won, the work of an advertising campaign can begin.

To help you understand what the advertising art director does, let's take a quick tour of an advertising agency and see just where the person who holds this position fits in.

Client and Agency Roles

First there is the client, and the client may be a large, medium-sized, or small commercial or industrial company—in other words, a soap manufacturer, a manufacturer of power tools or lawn mowers, or any one of the thousands of different businesses. This is the company that has hired the advertising agency to do its advertising. The project may be the introduction of a new product, it may be the advertising of a newly improved product, or it may be an advertising campaign to show the company in its best light (i.e., selling not the company's *product*, but the company's *public image*).

In this case, the client has developed the sales and marketing strategy for a product and has now given that strategy to the advertising agency to develop into an advertising campaign. Let's assume at this moment that the client, or advertiser, is a national company and wants the advertising campaign to include both television commercials and advertisements in national magazines and in local as well as national newspapers. All of these efforts will need to be coordinated.

As an art director in an advertising agency, you will now perform the following functions in connection with both the television campaign and the print campaign. To simplify matters, let's take each separately.

Print Art Direction

As an art director, you will first meet with the agency account executive to discuss the client's strategy. The account executive, by the way, is normally not involved in the creative process of the advertisement but is basically the manager of the account. This individual makes sure that all schedules are met, presents key campaigns to the client, and receives information from the client concerning these campaigns. The account executive is, in essence, a liaison between the advertising agency and the client. At the beginning of a print campaign, the account executive will meet with both the art director and the copywriter to discuss the overall creative strategy—the major selling points of the campaign and what must be emphasized in both print and television advertising.

Working with the Copywriter

As the art director on the account, you will have many meetings with the copywriter—the person in the agency who will be writing the headlines and the body copy for the advertisement. The chances are that the copywriter will first translate the client's creative strategy into words. Once the copywriter has developed a catchy or hard-sell line and has roughly developed the body copy—the main selling points of the strategy or product—he or she will then sit down with the art director. The art director will ask many questions concerning what must be emphasized and which points are more important than others. The art director then will begin to develop layout ideas for the ad.

Rough Layout

The art director will be responsible eventually for coming up with a rough layout. The rough layout will consist of the headline, space for the body copy (since in many cases the body copy will not have been completely resolved), and a general overall visual look for the advertisement. The art director may create a novel look—a photograph taken at an unusual angle, for example, or any other of a variety of means to develop an advertisement that will attract the reader of the magazine or newspaper, who, by the way, is the ultimate consumer. In some cases, the art director may specify an all-type advertisement in which there are no pictures or illustrations used but simply hard-hitting, bold type.

To help the art director in developing a rough layout, the agency may assign either a freelance sketch artist or a staff designer who will draw very rough pictures in the proper place under the direction of the art director. If an illustration is to be used, the art director may ask for a somewhat more finished piece of art, which will not be like the final art but will show the client what the idea is. A digital rough may also be composed on the computer using photographs found on stock photo websites or scanned from magazines. Just how finished the layout is depends a great deal on the importance of the client, what kind of an ultimate impression the agency wants to make, and how much money is available to do this. Once the rough layout has been developed, it is then given to the account executive, who eventually presents it to the client for approval.

Production

Once the client approves the rough layout (the concept), the art director then begins the production of the advertisement. If the advertisement is going to utilize a photograph, the art director will either call in portfolios from various photographers to select one who is appropriate to shoot this particular job, or find specific images from stock photography companies. At this time, the art director will also begin to pull together rough costs on using a photographer or stock photography and any other facets of the advertisement.

If an illustration is to be used, the same procedure will be followed, except that the portfolios of various commercial illustrators will be called in for evaluation. Eventually the art director, and possibly the client, will make the final decision concerning who will do the art or photography for the advertisement.

Work of the Production Department

In addition, the art director will meet with the production department, which is generally concerned with producing the ad. The production department will prepare the engraving plates for ultimate submission to the various magazines. Normally, since offset printing is used by most publications (except newspapers, which use the gravure and letterpress), film can be provided to the magazines that will publish the ad, and they will handle the printing. Even though the production department is responsible for ensuring the proper reproduction of the advertisements in the magazines or newspapers, the art director must be aware of the problems involved in the production of the advertisements.

Ongoing Projects

Once the advertisement has reached the production stage—when the photographs or illustrations have been completed and the production department has put together the mechanicals and the necessary plates—then the art director is usually working on the other projects. In smaller agencies, an art director may service several accounts and have a variety of projects going on simultaneously. In large agencies, often an art director is assigned to one major account and spends all of his or her time working on the ongoing projects for that account.

Television Art Direction

The art director who works in television is faced with a series of different challenges from those to be found working in print media. One main difference is that there is a great deal more money involved in television. For example, a single thirty-second ad can cost in the hundreds of thousands of dollars. Compare these costs to the tens of thousands for a print ad. Because the dollars are so great, there are usually more people involved in the production of a television commercial than there are in the production of a print ad.

Planning the Project

In general, the formula for planning a television ad is similar to that for planning a print ad. The client sets the objectives of the campaign, describing the product or service that must be sold and how it will be sold. The client gives this information to the account executive, who again passes it on to the creative department.

Scriptwriters or Copywriters

The copywriter, in general, will begin the process of a television commercial by writing the script. This script will outline the action that will take place and the words that will be spoken by the actors and actresses if live action is used. The preliminary script will serve as a guide to all the staff and freelance workers on the production team.

Storyboard Artists

Once the copywriter has completed this process and has received approval from the agency executive, the art director will take over and supervise the production of a storyboard. A storyboard is merely a series of small frames (usually twelve inches square) that graphically show the action that will take place on film. The storyboard normally will be produced by either a staff storyboard artist or a freelance storyboard artist. The storyboard artist will work with magic markers or sometimes with paint, depending on the sophistication of the client and the amount of money involved. In most cases, the art director will not get involved in the production of any storyboards, but will oversee the work.

Once a storyboard has been completed, the art director, at his or her discretion or at the discretion of the account executive, may also add a music track to help demonstrate for the client approximately what the commercial will sound like. Actors may be hired to speak the lines even though they may not be the final actors and actresses to be used in the commercial. At this point the storyboard is presented to the client for approval, and once approval is obtained, the storyboard is submitted to a television production house.

Television Production House

Television production houses specialize in filming television commercials both on videotape and on 16 and 35 millimeter film. A television production house usually employs a director, who is responsible for directing the actors, the camerawork involved on the television commercial, and the people who will control budget costs. Television production is heavily unionized; consequently, there is a great deal of paperwork involved with coordination between unions, the production house, and the client to avoid labor problems or any other problems that may arise. It is an accepted rule in advertising agencies that, usually, separate bids are taken from three different production houses for each television commercial. The producer will be responsible for approving those bids and making sure that all essential questions are answered.

Once the agency agrees to the bid price of the winning television production house, then the television commercial will be shot. The actual production of the television commercial, as well as the direction of the actors and the filming itself, will all be under the control of the television production house. However, the agency art director, along with the client, the account executive, and other agency personnel, will be present at the final shooting, and the art director will have the power to make key decisions concerning what happens in the commercial. In general, the commercial follows the approved storyboard very closely, but small decisions along the way must be made as the commercial is being filmed. A person or several people will be hired to do any voiceover work that the commercial needs. If music is used, an independent music firm will be hired. Once the film has been completed, the art director will work with the film editor to put together the final television print that will be released to the stations. Often a different firm that is not associated with the television production house edits the film.

Rewards and Outlook

It is easy to see that the majority of work in filming a television commercial is done by other people besides the art director, and that the art director's degree of absolute control is normally less than it would be in putting together a magazine or newspaper print advertisement. However, because of the tremendous sums of money spent in this medium, the art director who specializes in television may receive a much higher salary than does an art director who works only in print.

For those looking for top dollar, getting a good reel—a composite of all the television commercials the art director has worked on—is a vital part of the job search. Television art direction is exciting, stressful, demanding, creative, and often extremely lucrative, and with the addition of many new sophisticated cable networks to the market, it is growing every year.

Types of Advertising Agencies

The type of agency you work for will depend a great deal on the kind of advertising you are most interested in. For example, a large advertising agency in a metropolitan area probably will be very heavily involved in television. Most of its accounts will be major advertisers using television, magazine, and newspaper advertising. If you work for a larger advertising agency, you will usually be assigned to one major account with other art directors who will also be working on projects for the same account. Consequently, your autonomy will be limited, compared to what it would be with smaller agencies. However, the pay in large agencies is usually greater because the accounts are bigger and the opportunities for advancement to even larger accounts are greater also. In this case, the opportunity for more money and prestige are available to you.

On the other hand, many art directors go to work for small or medium-sized agencies that may not use any television advertising at all, instead pouring all of their client's advertising orders into consumer trade magazines and newspapers. Consumer advertising is that advertising geared to the retail consumer, while trade advertising is geared more toward the dealer or distributor customer. In the small and medium-sized agencies, it is quite possible that an art director will work on more than one account, thereby acquiring a great deal of diversified experience while also maintaining greater control over the kind of advertising that will be produced. The salaries may not be as high in smaller agencies, in most cases, but often the satisfaction is greater, which may be much more important to you.

Locations of Advertising Agencies

New York City is the mecca for all advertising agencies, and, therefore, it is the most competitive as well. There are large, medium, and small advertising agencies in New York; many of them are specialists in specific areas such as fashion, industrial, corporate, and pharmaceutical firms, as well as consumer agencies. The new art director has an excellent chance of finding work in some area or at some level. Other cities that have a major share of the larger consumer agencies include Atlanta, Chicago, Houston, and San Francisco. The key thing is that any city has one or two large advertising agencies, or at least a branch office of a major agency, as well as at least one smaller advertising agency that will work closely with local merchants and manufacturers. So in metropolitan areas, there is an opportunity at almost any level for the art director who is ambitious and ready to work.

Art Director Training Programs

In the early 1960s, when the economy was expanding and agency profits as well as corporate profits were up, most major advertising agencies had fairly extensive training programs for both advertising art directors and copywriters. It was possible for someone directly out of art school to take a job at a minimum wage and learn the business of art direction under the auspices of a formal advertising training program.

Unfortunately, with the recessions of the last two decades, most agencies abandoned their training programs. However, some training programs still exist on a minimal level, and these training programs offer a designer the chance to learn the advertising business by dealing directly with experienced art directors in the field.

If you are lucky enough to get into a company where one of these programs is in effect, take every advantage of it and learn all you can. The experience will serve you well later in your career.

Finding a Job as an Art Director

Generally, depending on the market, there are few new openings in art director jobs, and many, many people go after these few jobs. Most art director positions require several years of experience, and some companies will not even consider designers with fewer than two years of experience. If you choose to pursue an art director position coming out of art school, you must have a very impressive portfolio. The importance of a designer's portfolio cannot be overemphasized! Getting an art director's job basically involves knocking on doors and running down all leads, trying to convince someone that you are art director material.

The Advertising Agency Redbook

For a general list of the major advertising agencies, you should consult the *Standard Directory of Advertising Agencies*, which is published by the National Register Publishing Company. This book is available in major public and university libraries, and it contains the names, addresses, and phone numbers of all the major agencies in the country, as well as the key personnel and, most importantly, the accounts that the agencies handle. By consulting this book, a potential art director can "meet" an agency and find out how much that agency bills each year, its size, the number of its employees, the percentage of advertising in television versus print media that it uses, as well as the kinds of accounts (industrial, consumer, and so forth) that it handles. It is considered the "bible" of the advertising business. In addition, two weekly newspapers, *Advertising Age* and *Adweek*, are also "must" reading for any potential art director. They fully cover the advertising business—new trends, new companies, mergers and closings, account changes, personnel changes, success stories, and awards.

To sum up, being an art director provides an excellent opportunity to combine visual presentation and artistry with the art of selling. The art director is in essence a visual salesperson who takes the major selling points of a corporation or its products and translates them into advertising, public relations, and package design that ultimately creates the opportunity for more sales. The advertising art director, or public relations or packaging art director, is in the business of selling, and it is very important for anyone considering a career as an art director to understand that.

As Red Motley, one of the great salesmen for *Parade* magazine, once said: "Nothing happens until somebody sells something." And the art director, through visual communications, is able to make that sale happen, or at least create the atmosphere in which the sale can be closed. It is an honorable and exciting profession, and it can be a very profitable and interesting one as well.

4

More Opportunities in
Advertising Agencies and
Other Companies

THERE ARE MANY more opportunities for artists in advertising companies and other companies in addition to those involved in the art direction of major print and television campaigns. This chapter touches on some of these jobs.

Collateral Departments

Many advertising agencies and corporations have in-house departments or divisions that produce collateral material, which is something entirely separate from their general advertising business. Collateral material may be direct mail promotion pieces, small brochures that are mailed to customers by clients, special displays for retail stores, cooperative advertising ads, and company websites. The cost of local advertising is shared by both the dealer and the advertiser of co-op ads, the production of which may be done by the advertising agency, along with a variety of odds and ends that have nothing to do with advertising but do promote the overall advertising effort. All of this material requires an art director to design and oversee the production for best results. Some agencies employ art directors who specialize in the area of promotion, while in other agencies, general advertising art directors are assigned to handle all collateral materials.

Art Buyers

Many large agencies hire an art buyer, whose job is essentially to screen illustrator and photographer portfolios as well as control all the paperwork that results from the assignment of an advertising job, such as purchase orders, approvals, and model releases. In large agencies, there often are a number of art buyers, each responsible for a series of accounts. In smaller agencies, if an art buyer system is present, one art buyer may be responsible for all buying. In some companies, the art buyer has buying responsibility and can make the decision as to what talent is used. In other agencies, the art buyer will recommend certain talent to the art director, who will make the final decision. There are no rigid qualifications necessary to be an art buyer, but knowledge of art and photography, as well as agency experience and good organization and administration skills, are typically prerequisites.

Comp Artists

The comp artist is generally a staff artist who is responsible for producing various layouts for use by the art director in presentation to the client. These layouts may be created in a number of different media. In many cases, comp artists are excellent artists themselves but prefer the challenge of a variety of assignments. The important thing to remember is that the art produced by these comp artists is not finished art but is used for presentation purposes only. The name comes from the word *comprehensive*: a comprehensive layout is one that shows all of the elements that will appear in the final ad, in place, roughed in with approximate texture, color, line, and mass. The comp artist may work on a variety of projects in a week, including the projects for many different accounts. A comp artist must have the ability to draw, should know color, and should be extremely fast in whatever art medium is used. There is a certain amount of freelance comp work available, but every advertising agency maintains at least one comp artist on staff to handle this presentation work.

Storyboard Artists

As mentioned in Chapter 3, storyboard artists are staff or freelance artists who do nothing but storyboards for presentation to the client prior to the production of television commercials. The storyboard artist must be able to draw well, be fairly realistic in style, and be able to conceptualize quickly and translate that conception into miniature artwork in a very short period of time. Storyboards are usually done in color and, in many cases, the art style required is very realistic. Many storyboards are of excellent quality, depending on the client involved and the money to be spent. Others can be very rough in nature, again depending upon what is required by the circumstances.

For those who are interested in working steadily in an agency and receiving very good pay, the job of the storyboard artist represents an excellent opportunity. Good freelance storyboard artists can earn excellent fees, and advertising agencies that are heavily involved in television have an insatiable need for their work.

Layout and Pasteup Artists

For those companies that still utilize pasteup materials, the jobs of layout and pasteup artists are usually beginning positions for artists or illustrators fresh out of art school. Most of their work will be spent in what is called the agency "bullpen" and will consist primarily of making mechanicals. A *mechanical* is the workup of the ad that is required prior to the making of a plate for printing. Before 1960, most artists coming out of school worked in large art studios where they not only illustrated but also did pasteup and mechanical work. With the ease of computer layouts, the scope of these jobs has been lost, but every commercial artist should know these fundamentals. Most advertising agencies do still have a number of layout and pasteup artists on staff. These positions offer the beginning artist an opportunity to learn and eventually to move up within the agency to become assistants and art directors.

Assistant Art Directors

The assistant art director job can be an entry position in an agency. The assistant art director works under the direction of an established art director and learns generally how an art director functions within the structure. Eventually, the assistant art director will handle a certain amount of buying responsibility and, if his or her work is acceptable, will be made a full art director and be assigned to specific accounts.

Freelance Art Direction

There has been a recent trend toward hiring freelance art directors as opposed to having a salaried or on-staff advertising art director. In an effort to control overhead costs and to get maximum efficiency, many agencies are assigning certain projects to freelance or outside art directors. Usually a freelance art director is one who has had experience working on accounts similar to what the agency currently handles. The freelance art director charges by the project and is not on the agency's payroll. In many cases, the freelance art director supports the regular on-staff art directors, thus helping relieve the workload. To work effectively, the freelance art director should have years of agency exposure as a successful art director before becoming an independent contractor.

5

GRAPHIC DESIGN OPPORTUNITIES

A PERSON WHO is interested in designing rather than illustrating or photographing specific products has ample opportunity to do so through a variety of design outlets. Obviously, many of the job areas listed in this book utilize graphic designers either on a freelance basis or on staff to conceive and oversee a project from start to finish. The graphic designer has the eye to select and arrange type, art, and photos for layouts, books, or websites, to name a few. These tasks may be done in cooperation with the art director, artist, photographer, typesetter, account executive, and client; or, they may be carried out independently, depending on the size of the agency or corporation or the importance of the project.

Graphic Design Specialties

In addition to graphic design positions at newspapers, corporate advertising departments, movie studios, local television stations, and other businesses, there also are graphic design studios and other graphic design departments that offer excellent opportunities for the beginning designer. These graphic design firms may specialize in several of the following areas.

Annual Reports

A corporation is required by law to publish an annual report of the company, which includes its earnings, its product line, the names of its officers, its holdings, and other information. In some cases, a corporation with its own in-house design department will publish the annual report itself, but in many other cases, an outside graphic design studio will be contracted to handle this job. The designer will be responsible for developing the concept of the annual report as well as providing the necessary layouts, photographs, and charts and graphs of technical data so that the annual report can become a unified entity and do an effective job in selling the company. Annual reports have become more graphically appealing and creative in recent years. They are now some of the most exciting projects for designers.

Packaging

Packaging has become a fast-growing field because of the increase in marketing goods for impulse buying at the supermarket or other mass-merchandiser level. In essence, an effectively designed package becomes a self-contained and constant selling agent for the company. Graphic design studios that specialize in packaging provide an excellent opportunity for the person who is graphically oriented and who is able to develop an idea or concept into a packaging format for maximum impact on the customer. The person may start out as a simple layout artist and eventually move up to a position as a head graphic designer on specific packaging jobs. Packaging design studios can often work directly for corporations or through advertising agencies that have special packaging problems to solve for their clients.

Public Relations

Major public relations firms also have designers on staff. The difference between an advertising agency and a public relations firm is that the public relations firm usually promotes specific company policies, while the advertising agency promotes and advertises specific company products.

In a public relations firm, an art director may be involved in putting together an annual report, a company employee brochure, a company newspaper, or art for press releases and publicity campaigns, but most likely he or she will oversee a staff in the production of corporate materials.

Corporate Identification

Graphic designers also create corporate identification programs, which consist of the development of logos, trademark names, signs, letterheads systems, websites, or other collateral materials that are geared to unify and promote the overall company image. The redesign and renaming of Ameritech to SBC is an example of the tremendous work required in making such a changeover in a worldwide image. Companies are continually changing their images or their names as a result of new product lines or mergers with other companies, and the corporate identification field is becoming a very lucrative and challenging one for graphic designers that specialize in this area.

Music and Video

Thanks in large part to the advent of specialized cable television networks such as MTV, compact disc design is a very exciting area of graphic design. Most recording companies have an art director who is responsible for the overall graphic look of the CDs released by the company. In addition, these companies often have individual art directors responsible for certain areas, such as classical music, jazz, or rock.

Much of the conceptual work is done internally by either the art director or perhaps a staff designer or designers. However, freelance illustrators, under the direction of the art director or staff designer, can provide the illustrations or photography required for CD covers and booklets. The advantage of working for a record company (either on a staff or as a freelancer) is the tremendous variety in assignments. Music covers many different moods, and each mood requires a different kind of look or artistic feeling. Most freelance illustrators enjoy the opportunity to work with record companies precisely because of this artistic freedom.

Web Design

The Internet has flooded our culture, making it possible to access information with the click of a mouse. There has been an increasing trend in design to steer away from print design and into Web design. More computer-savvy designers are finding exciting opportunities for Web production, a field that is changing every day. Almost all companies nowadays have websites, and some have their own Web designers to maintain their sites and change their designs according to the times.

Design Studio

A design firm handles any of the aforementioned projects as part of their overall strategy but most often will handle the design of company brochures, stockholder reports, point-of-purchase displays, websites, or almost anything that needs to be printed or produced for the betterment or promotion of a company. For example, a corporate advertising department might hire a design firm to produce that corporation's sales promotion materials. The corporation may also hire a design firm to develop a special stockholder report, a special company brochure for its employees, or a variety of other projects that cannot be handled internally by the corporation. Designers who are responsible for specific projects staff the design studio. A project designer usually has overall responsibility for all aspects of the job. General design firms offer an excellent opportunity for freelance artists or photographers, since the studios utilize outside talent extensively in putting together their projects.

Art Studio

Closely allied to the design studio is the art studio. At one time, the art studio dominated the art field in all of the major metropolitan areas throughout the country, but now freelance artists have taken over most of the services provided by art studios. The initial function of the art studio was to provide art services to corporations, advertising agencies, and others by maintaining a staff of artists on its premises. The studio also acted as the sales agent for these artists. In fact, the essential difference between the graphic design studio and the art studio has always been the way the work is contracted: graphic design studios utilize either designers on staff or freelance talent and pay a fee to these freelancers for the services performed. An art studio provides studio space to artists and also acts as the selling agent for these artists. The art studio, in general, has become a thing of the past and at the moment does not represent many opportunities for the person interested in a career in art. However, design firms—particularly those that are interested in the whole area of graphic design—do represent a growing and lucrative area and should be thoroughly investigated.

Animation Studio

The animation studio provides art for animated commercials as well as animation for corporate and network graphics. Graphics for television stations have become one of the major target areas for animation studios, and they are replacing the animated commercial as a prime source of income in this area.

Animation studios or houses generally work in the following manner:

1. A storyboard is provided to the animation house by an advertising agency, at which point the animation house bids on the board, giving the agency an estimate of how much it would cost to produce the thirty- or sixty-second commercial in an animated form.

2. If the animation studio gets the project, the first step is to obtain key art. Key art is those pieces of art that show the pre-

dominant action in the commercial. There may be, for example, as many as six, eight, or ten pieces of key art, with each piece of art perhaps showing a character, a key piece of action, or some other element. This key art may be produced by a staff artist at the animation studio or may be freelanced to an outside illustrator.

3. Once the key art has been completed, the animation studio then turns it over to a series of animators who are on staff at the animation studio. These animators literally make the key art move, matching the art style exactly and drawing or painting every single movement to be made in the commercial. Obviously, animation artists are excellent talents who intentionally choose to do this kind of work, instead of becoming freelance illustrators or other kinds of artists.

4. Once the animation artwork has been completed, then the entire concept is transferred to film and goes into production as an animated commercial.

Obviously, anyone who is interested in animated art and has the artistic talent to produce it will find a challenging and lucrative opportunity in these animation studios, many of which are located in New York or southern California and are closely allied to the television and film industries.

6

Book Publishing Market

THEY SAY NEVER judge a book by its cover. But a book cover can become a selling point for a publishing company, and the opportunities in the book publishing business are tremendous. It is important to understand that there are several different areas of book publishing, all of which have different requirements and opportunities for the person interested in a career in this area.

Trade Books

Trade publishing houses publish both hardcover and paperback books that are sold through bookstores throughout the country. These books may be bestselling novels, fiction and nonfiction books, children's books, special-interest books, or books covering a variety of consumer and technical subjects. The essential thing to understand is that all of the books are provided through independent, or in some cases, company-owned or company-financed, bookstores across the country, so the distribution is very carefully controlled. Major publishing houses provide opportunities for people interested in being art directors and designers. Each line of books that is published by a company might have an individual art director responsible for the design and graphics of the books in that line. The publisher also needs book designers to create the covers and interiors of the books. The person seeking a job in publishing obviously should enjoy reading books and should be interested in providing the best kind of format for the sale of books.

Art Director's Role

The art director at a publishing company is generally responsible for the overall design of all of the books as well as the purchasing of cover art and photography from outside illustrators and photographers.

Staff Designers

In addition to the art director, the publisher will often have a group of staff designers who will be responsible for specifying type, creating covers and interiors on the computer, and generally overseeing the production of the books.

Educational Publishers

Educational publishers provide textbooks and other learning materials to schools on all levels throughout the country. They use outside illustrators and photographers to provide much of the artwork for the tremendous volume of inexpensive and yet vital books to grammar schools, high schools, and colleges. In addition, these educational publishers have fairly significant staffs of designers, artists, and typesetters. The volume of the materials supplied to schools can be enormous. In some cases, educational publishers pay higher salaries than do other types of publishing companies.

Commercial artists have the advantage of developing long-term relationships for work on series of books and other visual print materials. These projects can often mean work for many months or even years for textbooks, guides, and other components.

Paperback Books

Obviously, paperback books are dominating the publishing business today. Paperback publishers often can be a subsidiary or a separate division of another major publisher. The paperback publishing house can also be a completely independent company that publishes nothing but paperbacks. Paperbacks are sold through bookstores and other traditional channels of book distribution or through mass merchandising outlets such as airports, drugstores, and supermarkets, with much of the distribution often being handled by independent magazine and newspaper distributors.

Nature of the Market for Art

Paperbacks represent a tremendous opportunity for the freelance artist or photographer because some of the major publishers create as many as four hundred covers a month, all of which will use either artwork or photography. Generally the style of art required for most of the paperback work is photo-realism. The subject matter in paperbacks can vary from historical romance to action to contemporary romance to general interest books, so the staff or freelance illustrator/photographer has the opportunity to provide a great variety of art for a business that is rapidly increasing in volume in this country.

Freelance Work

The publishing area also represents an excellent opportunity for the freelance artist, since all of the books require cover art and, in many cases, inside illustrations. The freelancer who can both write and illustrate children's books, for example, may find publishers an excellent vehicle for getting books published and distributed. Freelance designers are hired to design the cover and interior layouts for publishing companies when the staff designers' workload gets too high.

Many book publishers tend to be conservative in taste and market approach, but they represent a very important part of the commercial art market.

Book Packagers

A fairly recent phenomenon in the book industry is the book packager. Book packagers are companies that write the story; do the book design, art, and photography; and produce the total book from start to finish for sale to another publisher for distribution. These book packagers can provide this kind of service more efficiently and sometimes less expensively than can a publishing house. The book packagers utilize freelance writers, artists, designers, and a variety of other services to put together a book. They represent a new and growing opportunity in the publishing field.

Specialized Publishers

There are hundreds of specialized publishers throughout the country, some of them consisting of a husband-and-wife team who publish perhaps only a few books a year that are special in nature and require art and design services of some kind. A steady reading of a magazine like *Publishers Weekly* can acquaint the person interested in opportunities in publishing with information on where the publishers are, the kinds of books they publish, and often the requirements needed to publish these books.

There are also very large special-interest publishers that offer opportunities to the person interested in art direction and graphic design. These special areas also offer an excellent opportunity to the freelance illustrator, since they use a wide variety of art styles such as special historical books, "how-to" books, one-of-a-kind collectible books, and condensed novels. In addition, special-interest publishers often have merchandising divisions that also produce commemorative plates, CD and cassette covers, and other special promotions. These divisions not only use freelance talent but also maintain a fairly significant staff of art directors and designers to produce these various merchandising materials.

7

EDITORIAL DESIGN: MAGAZINES AND NEWSPAPERS

WORKING AS A graphic designer or artist for magazines and newspapers can offer some very different experiences to newcomers as well as established professionals. Here is a description of what it would be like to work in these publishing areas.

Magazine Publishing

Magazine publishing is a very exciting part of the graphic design field. Consequently, the competition is intense in this area, especially with the top magazines in the New York City area. Your chances of getting even an entry-level job with a major magazine are slim if you apply directly out of school. Sometimes, however, the direct route is not the best or only route to a career in magazine publishing.

Drawing

One skill that prospective artists must learn as a means of gaining access to the magazine publishing field is the ability to draw. Every art department of every magazine has a frequent need for simple, quick drawings, or for someone to retouch an existing drawing, and they do not have the time to send the project out or hire a freelancer to do it. The project has to be done in-house by someone on staff. A person with the ability to do uncomplicated drawings or the ability to retouch someone else's drawings will always be in demand. Again, drawing ability is definitely a plus, but a designer will also scan existing images into a computer for quick, rough, magazine layouts.

Although applicants should try for jobs at a top magazine, they'll probably find other openings by approaching some of the house organs or trade publications. A house organ is a magazine that a company publishes for its employees, and these magazines usually employ art directors. Many professional associations (accountants', architects', bankers' associations, and so forth) also put out magazines especially for people in their trade areas and they, too, employ art directors. Then there are also many small and specialized publishers that employ art directors. These are all good places to start getting the experience and knowledge you need about the publishing field to help you go for the better jobs a little later on.

Portfolios

What does the entry-level person show in a portfolio? The more experienced person has garnered materials from other positions and can produce samples of all of the pieces he or she has art directed.

But what about the person just starting out of school or starting a new career? What does the newcomer show in a portfolio?

You will have to make up for lack of experience by composing a portfolio of student work or samples of how you would have handled the design of a particular magazine page or cover. Publishers want to get an idea of how your thinking relates to the product they're putting out, so you should include a variety of pieces related to the kind of job you're aiming for.

One art director now at a major magazine designed sample pages for a women's magazine, did the type, cut the illustrations and photographs out of foreign women's magazines (so that everything would be unrecognizable and fresh), and produced his own sample layouts for his portfolio. This gave the editors of the women's magazine he was applying to some idea of how he would design pages in their magazine. He got an entry-level position doing pasteups and mechanicals—a small start, but at least a job. Today he is an art director, because once he got in, he was able to work his way up.

The beginner is going to have to use ingenuity in putting together a portfolio. Remember that prospective employers want to know what you'll contribute to their business as an employee, and so you are going to have to design a portfolio to get this idea across. In assembling your portfolio, research your product, especially the company you want to work for, and then design the portfolio with that company in mind.

Staff Hierarchy

What are some of the positions on a magazine staff? Usually a person starting out at the bottom of an art department will mainly do pasteups and mechanicals and virtually anything that no one else wants to do. Once beyond these entry-level jobs, an artist will start handling better articles and maybe even will manage and assign a few freelance jobs with limited budgets.

Depending on the size of the company, there may be as many as five or six steps to take until an artist becomes an executive art director or executive art designer. The position below the executive art director or designer level is usually the associate or assistant art director or designer. When an artist arrives at this level, he or she will have many responsibilities, including handing out numerous freelance assignments and selecting which artists' and photographers' and designers' work will appear in the magazine. This is important because what the art director or designer selects will in turn affect the look of the magazine. He or she also may oversee subordinates on the art staff.

The executive or senior art director or designer is, as the name implies, an executive. The senior art director or designer has, in addition to the full financial and personnel administration of the art department, total responsibility for the look and design of the finished product. Although it sounds like this job has more to do with business than with art, this senior position also entitles its holder to choose and work with some of the top commercial talents in the world, which can go a long way toward providing personal satisfaction on the job.

Freelancing

Every magazine uses the talents of freelancers to some degree to put out its product. The in-house art department will decide whether a story needs an illustration or a photograph to highlight it. Once that determination is made, the art department decides on what type of photography or illustration is required, and then an artist, photographer, or other specialist is given the job.

Because freelancers are hired on an assignment-to-assignment basis, the fees they are paid are usually good. At the top levels, these fees often can range into the thousands of dollars for a day's or sometimes a few hours' work. Because of the potential in income, the top jobs in freelance work are eagerly sought, especially those jobs with the major magazines, where the fees are usually the highest. This is why in markets like New York City, where a majority of the leading magazines are headquartered, the market is one of the most competitive in the world.

There are, of course, many moderate and lower-paying freelance jobs. A good rule of thumb is to consider the dollar volume of the business involved. Large-circulation national magazines will usually pay more than smaller, low-circulation publications.

Getting Assignments

What are the requirements to become a freelancer in the magazine field? To begin with, you'll have to start calling on art directors in the area and getting assignments in order to get a portfolio together. This may sound simple, but it is not. You must have the right style, be knowledgeable about what the marketplace is buying, and be prepared to support yourself for at least a year while you work up some accounts.

On the positive side, however, a freelancer does not have to be a graduate of an art school, does not need to have a résumé or credentials, and does not have to maintain high overhead. If your work has the look that the magazine is searching for, and if you can deliver that look, on time and consistently, you can get assignments. If you happen to work in a style that is in demand, the fees that can be earned in freelancing are dazzling. A good freelancer can make more than the president of a major corporation. Also, there is no age, sex, racial, or religious discrimination. If you have a style that is in demand, no one cares about who or what you are or how old you are. They simply want you to deliver.

The competition in this field is fierce. Only about one in a hundred freelancers can manage to make a living at the business, and only about one in a thousand becomes truly successful.

That said, don't forget that the major magazines are not the only sources of freelance work. Trade publications and company magazines are also sources of temporary employment. They don't pay as much, but a freelancer can often do well with more low-paying jobs on a steady basis than with one or two high-paying jobs that only come along once a year. Since the competition for these freelance assignments isn't as fierce, it is frequently the best place to start.

Newspaper Design

Newspapers provide many job opportunities for the freelance or staff designer or artist. The size of the newspaper and where it is located, whether it is a big city daily like the *New York Times* or the *Chicago Tribune* or a small hometown weekly newspaper, will determine the numbers and kinds of opportunities available.

Some of the opportunities available on a newspaper are as follows:

• Most large city newspapers have art directors who are responsible on a daily basis for all of the graphics that determine the "look" of the newspaper. Although this person might be known by different titles at some very small newspapers, someone has to be responsible for putting together the layout, the type, the photography, and the illustrations in any newspaper, large or small. The position may be more clearly defined on a much larger newspaper, but the position will still exist in some form no matter how small the newspaper.

• On the staffs of larger newspapers, often each section of the newspaper will have a separate art director. The individual art directors will be responsible for the layout, buying illustrations and photography, and assembling the individual sections for each day or weekend, depending on when the newspaper section comes out.

• The larger newspapers often will put an artist on staff, and this artist will be responsible for illustrating special features or special sections. In addition, the newspaper may also maintain a cartoonist on staff who can provide humorous or satirical illustrations.

• Some newspapers may still have artists to do pasteups and mechanicals for their publications, but in most cases, graphic designers will be hired to design the newspaper layouts on the computer. Newspaper turnaround is so fast and deadlines are so tight that digital production has become the more fast and effective norm. In smaller areas, the newspaper often serves as the sole advertising medium for local businesses and consequently will provide many design and art services that would normally be provided by other outside suppliers in larger metropolitan areas.

• Larger newspapers will maintain photographers on staff to perform special assignments such as covering news stories and to provide product photography for the various sections of the newspaper. For example, for the "Home" section of most newspapers, the staff photographer may be sent out to shoot a variety of interiors of finely decorated homes. The same might be done for a new product that is being discussed by a staff or freelance feature writer, and the accompanying photography will be provided by a newspaper staff photographer.

• Both magazines and newspapers will have Web designers on staff whose sole job is to maintain the online versions of the printed products. Almost every magazine and newspaper provides its publication online for its readers.

Newspapers represent an excellent opportunity for the freelance artist as well. Many newspapers, particularly those in the large metropolitan areas, use a tremendous amount of illustration, all of which lasts for exactly one day, which is the life of each daily newspaper. Most of this illustration work is black-and-white and must be done within extremely tight deadlines. Because the staff artist on the newspaper cannot handle the tremendous volume of work necessary, an outside freelance artist will, from time to time, be contracted to do various kinds of work for the newspaper. The section art director or the overall art director for the newspaper is the person to contact if you are looking for illustration assignments from the newspaper.

In addition to the previously mentioned assignments, the freelance artist should concentrate on those various advertising accounts that are heavily newspaper-oriented. For example, it is possible to do a great deal of illustration work directly with department stores in various cities. Although a department store may maintain a design and illustration staff to handle daily work, specialized illustration is often needed for particular promotions, and outside illustrators will be used. In addition, there are other accounts handled by advertising agencies, such as food store accounts, that use a tremendous number of black-and-white newspaper illustrations and provide more freelance job opportunities for the artist in these specialized areas.

Sales Promotion Division

Many large metropolitan newspapers maintain their own sales promotion department, which is entirely separate from the news reporting aspects of the paper. Art directors or designers generally staff the sales promotion division and as such, they are responsible for:

• Putting together specific promotions geared to attracting potential advertisers to the newspaper. These promotions may vary from the development of flipchart presentations for use by the newspaper's salespeople when contacting potential advertisers to direct mail brochures that will be mailed out by the newspaper to large segments of the advertising community.

• Providing specialized services to advertisers currently in the newspaper. For example, a particular advertiser may want some assistance in developing a specific merchandising or sales promotion program that extols the virtues of the advertising program currently running in the newspaper to send to its customers.

Sales promotion divisions of newspapers will often do much of the conception and layout work themselves, but they will also call upon freelancers to provide much of the illustration and photography.

Newspapers can represent a tremendous opportunity for the beginning artist or potential art director to learn an exciting business that is fast-paced and offers a variety of challenges on a daily basis. Although, realistically speaking, the pay on a newspaper may not be as much as that paid in an advertising agency or a corporation, often the benefits, challenges, and stimulation can far outweigh the financial benefits in other fields. Newspapers are the lifeblood of the communications industry in this country, and people working on a newspaper, no matter what the capacity, can always pride themselves on working for an institution that serves an extremely useful and vital function in our American way of life.

8

TELEVISION AND FILM MARKETS

TELEVISION HAS BECOME the biggest advertising medium in the world today, and it continues to grow thanks to the advent of cable television both nationally and internationally. Job opportunities in television are also rapidly expanding, and although they are highly competitive, these positions offer an excellent opportunity for growth, both financially and creatively.

There are several different areas in television that should be investigated by anyone contemplating a career in art.

Local Television

Almost every area in this country has at least one television station that services its residents, and these local television stations offer an opportunity for the person interested in art to become a part of television programming. The size of the station will have a great deal to do with the number of positions available.

Station Art Directors

In large metropolitan areas, someone will be responsible for a graphics staff, and that person will have the job title of art director. In smaller stations the titles may vary, but one person will be responsible for all on-air graphics such as station-break slides, titles, illustrations, special films, and anything else concerned with providing the visual involvement for on-air programs. On-air graphics has grown from the person holding up the hand-painted sign in front of the television camera to sophisticated use of computer animation and other techniques that make this field one of the fastest-growing anywhere, and certainly one of the most creative and challenging.

Staff Designers/Artists

The local station that does not have a full graphics department probably will have at least one person on staff who will be an illustrator or a combination illustrator/designer. Local television stations require a tremendous amount of graphic material, since most stations are on all day and into the night and have numerous station breaks, all of which require some form of graphic presentation. In addition, of particular interest to the graphic artist are the news shows, which rely heavily on computer animation and graphics. Graphics needed for news programs are very fast paced and often have to be done at the last minute. Some graphics may have to be created digitally minutes before they air!

This particular career area—the local television station—is not a very lucrative one for the freelance artist, although on occasion, particularly in the smaller stations, the freelance artist will have a chance to contribute artwork to the programming. In large metropolitan areas, staff artists and designers will do much of the work.

Graphics staffs for large local metropolitan television stations can be quite extensive and will only occasionally need freelance help.

Network Television

The three major national television networks, as well as some very large independent stations, are located in New York City. The three major networks—NBC, ABC, and CBS—maintain extensive internal art and design departments. These internal art departments consist of a number of art directors and designers responsible for particular areas of network programming. These areas include:

1. Advertising on a national level for major network television shows. Advertising in *TV Guide* and other major magazines will be done by an outside advertising agency hired by the network. Many consumer advertisements for the network that run in local newspapers throughout the country will be conceived and developed by internal network art departments.

2. Support material for all the local television affiliates. This material may be in the form of full-color posters, black-and-white newspaper ads, or special-promotion flyers. This material is provided to local network affiliates throughout the country for use in advertising the network shows at the local level.

Although the conception and ultimate development of these support materials will be done internally, the actual illustrations may be done by freelance artists.

3. Material for station-break slides, special-effects slides, and other items for use by both local stations (particularly in large metropolitan areas where the local station is closely affiliated with the network) and affiliates throughout the country.

Both the local television station and network art departments will maintain a photographic department that will provide the photography for use in network and local newspaper advertising, as well as publicity shots of the various newscasters, special guest/host photos, and other special promotional material.

Cable Television

Cable television is another field of opportunity for the person who is interested in an art career in television. Cable markets such as HBO, Showtime, MTV, VH1, Lifetime, and Nickelodeon are just some of the providers of movies and special entertainment. Cable television production is becoming just as sophisticated as network television; it utilizes many of the same services and requirements and has become a fast-growing market. These networks also have their own design facilities with in-house art departments that need both freelance and staff designers.

Film Industry

Today more than ever there are opportunities for the movie-oriented artist or potential art director to gain fame and fortune working in the movie business.

There are generally three separate areas that represent the best opportunities for the creative or artistic person looking for a career in the movie industry. These areas are in studio art direction, promotion, and freelance.

Studio Art Directors

The function of the studio art director and his or her staff, including artists and designers, is to provide art direction for the movies, titles on screen, and other graphic effects that are important to the movie as a whole. Jobs in studio art direction are extremely competitive, are difficult to obtain, and are highly coveted.

In addition to working for movie studios directly, there is considerable opportunity for the freelance movie art director to get work with independent filmmakers, performing the essential art direction functions that once were the prerogative only of the large movie studios in Hollywood.

Promotion

Movie promotion is by far the largest area for opportunities for the potential artist or art director. There are four distinct areas where these opportunities exist.

Ad Agency

Specialized advertising agencies or separate divisions of large advertising agencies are specifically set up to advertise and promote movies to the general public. These specialized agencies have art directors and graphic designers on staff. They provide a total advertising package, including the official movie poster used at the theater, the newspaper advertisements used in the local newspaper, special promotions used in magazines and other consumer publications, and the official movie website. In addition, these special advertising agencies will also get involved in major television advertising campaigns of movies, which are a major force in the promotion of movies to the general public.

Boutiques

Special boutiques also offer an opportunity in film art. These boutiques are set up in a form similar to specialized advertising agencies, but they do not handle the same volume of work and they generally restrict themselves to the development of the movie poster concept or website development.

Studio Advertising Departments

Because of the tremendous increase in the number of independent filmmakers, the large film company advertising department is slowly becoming a thing of the past. However, those that remain utilize the same kinds of artists that any corporate advertising department would utilize. The major difference is that the end product being advertised is a movie instead of a consumer product.

Title Companies

There are companies that specialize in the titles for movies. These companies generate the graphics for the beginning credits of the film that introduce the movie, as well as the ending credits. This used to be done by painting the lettering on glass and then photographing the glass over film. Now, the computer has replaced this glass-painting technique.

Freelance Work

Most of the illustrations used for movie posters and local advertising have been done by outside freelance illustrators working directly for the studio or the special advertising agency or boutique. The film industry is by far the most competitive of any field for commercial artists. Often several illustrators will compete for one movie poster assignment. The money available to a freelancer can be significant, and of course the thrill of seeing his or her poster art prominently displayed throughout the country at major theaters or in local newspapers is an added fringe benefit.

9

CORPORATE ART DEPARTMENTS AND PROMOTION DEPARTMENTS

ALMOST EVERY LARGE corporation has an advertising and sales promotion department, or in-house art department, that offers an excellent opportunity for a designer. One advantage of an in-house agency is greater control of the advertising program and its costs. A disadvantage of the in-house design department is the lesser opportunity to obtain independent thought and strategies and the benefit of the experience an outside advertising agency gains by servicing a variety of clients in a variety of industries. The department may vary from a one- or two-person department, particularly in the industrial and trade area, to a large number of artists, designers, copywriters, and other team members in the major consumer-oriented corporations such as cosmetics and clothing manufacturers. The corporate art and sales promotion department handles a number of projects and areas of responsibility.

Responsibilities of Corporate Advertising and Sales Promotion Departments

The advertising and sales promotion department is responsible for the corporation's advertising programs. The development and execution of these programs may ultimately be done by an outside advertising agency. In this case, the outside agency will provide counsel and a final product to promote the corporation's products. Often the in-house art department's management will be responsible for choosing the outside advertising agency and will work closely with this agency in the development and execution of all corporate advertising plans.

Collateral Materials

The advertising and sales promotion department also manages the development and final execution of advertising collateral materials. Advertising collateral materials are items such as the website, in-store displays, consumer brochures, posters, samplers, contests, and anything else that supports the overall corporate advertising program. These materials are generally developed and produced under the auspices of the corporate in-house advertising department.

Local Advertising

The conception, execution, and overall responsibility for local advertising programs in support of specialized local markets is also the responsibility of this department. These advertising campaigns generally are newspaper-oriented, and the advertising department independent of the separate advertising agencies may produce the ads for these programs.

Cooperative Ad Programs

Another responsibility of the corporate advertising and promotion department is that of the corporation's cooperative advertising programs. The corporation usually will provide matching funds to a local retailer or distributor if that retailer or distributor advertises the corporation's products on a local level. For example, under a typical cooperative advertising agreement, if a local retailer provides $5,000 worth of advertising in the town newspaper or local television station, the corporation may provide an additional $5,000 to increase advertising awareness in that area. The cooperative advertising agreement usually also entails the provision of actual advertising materials that can be used in the local newspaper, as well as the administration of all funds allocated to the cooperative advertising program.

Sampling Programs

If a corporation provides samples of its products to retailers, distributors, and other customers, the advertising and promotion department would handle the sampling of these products.

Market Research

Any market research test connected with the corporation's advertising and sales promotion programs would be administered by the corporate advertising department. Again, outside research firms could be used to conduct the actual research, but the responsibility and administration would still be under the control of the corporate advertising department.

Sales Support

The corporate advertising department provides local support for the corporation's sales force and its customers. This might include local in-store display programs, special promotions, and other programs developed by local corporate sales management working with independent retailers and distributors. The corporate advertising department would provide in-store banners, displays, and a variety of other promotional materials to make the promotion successful.

Sales Incentive Programs

Any incentive programs for salespeople, retailers, or distributors of the corporation such as sales contests and the providing of gifts, trips, and other forms of incentives will be planned and administered by the advertising department. In some cases, an independent firm specializing in incentives may be contracted to handle the administration of the contest, but the responsibility of the program still rests with the corporate advertising department.

Sales Meeting Presentations

In general, sales meetings for corporate sales forces or customers of a corporation are also a responsibility of the corporate advertising department. Specialized sales meeting firms may actually develop the sales meeting, but the responsibility for putting on the sales meetings and participating in them will rest with the advertising department. In connection with this, the advertising department management will play a large part in presenting the corporate advertising and sales promotion plans to the corporate sales force as a means of creating excitement for products and policies. Artists will design charts, graphs, audiovisual programs, and other materials for these presentations.

Institutional Advertising

The corporate advertising department is also responsible for developing institutional advertising on behalf of the corporation. Institutional advertising is that advertising that does not specifically sell any product manufactured by the corporation, but instead sells the image of the corporation to investors and the financial community, or creates goodwill for the corporation in the minds of the consumer. An advertising agency may develop the specific themes for corporate institutional advertising, but it would be directly responsible to the corporate advertising department.

In other words, the corporate advertising department would handle any activity that is connected to the advertising and promoting of either the corporation itself or the products of the corporation. This department calls upon outside suppliers such as printers, advertising agencies, sales meeting firms, and other specialists to help carry out the programs, but the ultimate responsibility for the success of all advertising and sales promotion programs rests with the corporate advertising department.

Corporate Advertising Department Staff

The size of an advertising department will obviously dictate the number and kinds of positions available in that department. However, in general, the following positions are found in a typical advertising department.

Advertising Managers/Directors

The head of the corporate advertising department is the advertising manager or director. This individual has the ultimate responsibility for administering the corporate advertising and sales promotion program. The manager or director will also have responsibility for its execution, its evaluation, and its budget. The corporate advertising manager—or advertising director, depending on which title is used—generally reports to a vice president of marketing in the larger corporations and sometimes directly to the president in smaller corporations.

Assistant Advertising Directors

The assistant advertising director is in effect a number-two person who is responsible for carrying out the policies of the corporate advertising manager and for working to develop and execute all of the corporate advertising programs. The assistant advertising manager reports directly to the corporate advertising manager.

Advertising Production Managers

The advertising production manager is responsible for producing all of the collateral materials, such as sales brochures, websites, point-of-purchase displays, samplers, and any other sales promotion material produced by the advertising department. The advertising production manager works with a number of outside suppliers such as printers, design studios, and freelancers, all of whom provide specialized services in producing the sales promotion material necessary to do an effective corporate selling job. The advertising production manager generally does not participate in the initial concept of the program, although his or her expertise is always needed in determining the most effective, inexpensive, and efficient ways to produce the sales promotion collateral materials. The advertising production manager usually reports to the corporate advertising manager.

Staff Designers

In the case of large corporate advertising departments, there may be several staff designers who are responsible for developing and following through on the final production of various sales promotion materials. In some cases, outside design studios may be brought in to develop promotional concepts, or the work may be done in-house by staff designers.

Staff Photographers

In some cases, a corporate advertising department may include a staff photographer, who will do a great deal of shooting of products for use in sales brochures and displays. Photography can also be freelanced to independent photographers, but to minimize cost and also maintain more efficient production, a photographer may be on a corporate manager's staff.

Display Managers

Often, corporations heavily involved in selling products through retailers to the consumer may keep a display manager on staff. This individual's responsibility will include developing and producing specialized in-store displays for use by retailers. For example, the display manager may develop concepts for window displays, wall displays, counter displays, and product sampling, all of which will be needed by the local retailers to display and sell the corporation's products. The display manager may have an assistant and even a special display designer working under his or her direction, depending on the scope, needs, and size of the corporation. The display manager will report to the manager or director of the advertising department.

Newcomer Advantages

There are several advantages to working for a corporate design department as compared to working for an advertising agency, magazine publisher, or other business:

1. As a member of the corporate advertising department—depending on the status of the employee within the department and his or her length of service—the person has an opportunity to participate in the full and complete advertising and promotion programs of the corporation instead of being isolated or restricted to one specific area, such as advertising, sales promotion, or displays. An overview of the total advertising and sales promotion picture is usually possible when working in a department.

2. There is continuity in a corporate advertising department that is not found in other areas. For example, it is possible in an advertising department to work for an entire year on plans for one major corporate advertising and sales promotion strategy, with all the efforts being exclusively directed toward the success of this program. In an independent advertising agency, by comparison, it is quite likely that the employee may work on a variety of programs and that his or her efforts may be diluted, depending on the time limitations for working on each account.

3. The pressure of working in a corporate advertising department is considerably less, and the job security generally better, than

that found in working for an advertising agency. In an advertising agency, accounts come and go and each has an effect upon the number of employees either hired or fired. There is much more stability on the corporate advertising department's side than that found in an agency.

4. The opportunity exists within a corporate advertising department to try a variety of functions or positions and to gain experience in many areas. For example, the corporate employee may find that he or she enjoys making presentations at sales meetings, which is something that might not be possible working for an advertising agency or a magazine.

In general, the pay scale in a corporate design department is somewhat higher than that offered in an advertising agency or in publishing. This is in addition to a more stable work environment, better benefits, and a greater variety of challenges than are often found in other career areas.

10

OTHER SPECIAL CAREER OPPORTUNITIES

CAREERS IN COMMERCIAL art and graphic design are not limited to advertising, publishing, corporate, or television and film companies. There are many other fascinating areas where a graphic artist can put his or her talents to work. This chapter examines some of these opportunities.

Architectural and Interior Design Firms

Architectural and interior design companies are very different from the usual graphic design studio in two major ways: they specialize in exterior and interior architecture, and this service is primarily for commercial and industrial firms rather than for private home owners. These architectural design firms present an excellent opportunity for the artist or art director with a special knack for architectural renderings. Much of the artist's work done for these firms deals with carrying out in drawings the ideas of the architect and the client.

In addition, the person who enjoys interior design—which is laying out office or institutional space to maximize its use for the most efficient flow of traffic, to make the most practical use of the space, and to achieve the most pleasing effects visually—has available many additional career opportunities.

Both architectural and interior design firms utilize model makers, mural artists, sculptors, stained glass artists, and other special artists and craftspeople who can provide decoration and artistic emphasis for their buildings. These art firms are important sources of work for both freelancers and staff artists and designers.

Retail Design Firms

Retail design firms are full-service design firms that consist of architects, planners, interior designers, art directors, and graphic designers. All of these people will work together to design a retail store or restaurant for a client. Architects will design the space; interior designers will decide how the space works; and art directors and graphic designers will design signage and any other business collateral the client may need. These firms are an exciting opportunity to do great work and be able to see your work come to life.

Greeting Card Companies

The greeting card industry is a large one in this country and has for generations been dominated by Hallmark Cards (located in Kansas City), which uses the services of hundreds of artists. Hallmark and companies like it hire staff artists and designers who are primarily charged with the responsibility of developing new design and conceptual ideas for complete greeting card lines, stationery, party supplies, and other graphic materials.

One thing that the aspiring artist should remember is that major card companies such as Hallmark rely almost exclusively on in-house artists to produce the many greeting cards and related products of the company. Smaller greeting card companies utilize more freelance talent. *Greetings, Etc.* (see Appendix B) provides information about the trade and is "must" reading for this market.

Specialty Cards

In addition to Hallmark greeting cards, there has been a recent trend in more specialized greeting cards and announcements. Many freelance designers and illustrators and calligraphers are making their living designing cards, invitations, and birth announcements, to name a few. Artists sell these specialty items in special stores, through websites, or by custom order.

Printers

Many large printers maintain a design or art studio as a means of servicing their clients. For example, in some cases printers will handle an entire sales promotion project from start to finish, including the concept of a brochure, the design of the brochure, type specifications, taking of the photographs, and final production in printing. The printer may employ a staff artist, a staff designer, or a freelance artist to do thumbnail sketches and mechanicals. When you are looking for a job in a particular area, you should survey local printers to find out whether they maintain a full design or art studio on staff, or whether mechanicals, designs, and engravings are provided by outside suppliers.

Agents

One of the job opportunities that is generally unrecognized by the field, but that can be an extremely lucrative profession, is that of an agent (often called a *rep*). The agent, who operates as an independent contractor, represents commercial illustrators, photographers, and in some cases, fine artists, and sells their services to galleries, corporations, and other businesses. For the artist who is as much of a businessperson and salesperson as an artist, becoming a representative can be an excellent way to combine both artistic interests and business sense in a successful career. No real formal training is required to become an artist's representative, although a background in art and sales is helpful. However, this is not absolutely required, and many successful representatives in the field have come from other areas and have been able to do extremely well. Agents can also work at artist staffing agencies that specialize in finding work for other artists and designers.

Being an artist's representative—representing artists either on an exclusive or nonexclusive basis—can be an exciting career for the artist who also enjoys selling and working with people. Many artists represent themselves when they are starting out and are able to see firsthand the advantages and disadvantages of selling in the open marketplace. Often as artists become more successful, they require representatives to handle the selling for them. There is presently an urgent need for agents, since the number of freelance artists in the field far outweighs the number of agents available to represent them.

Fashion Market

Fashion is always "in" or "out," and the person who enjoys fast-paced advertising, art direction, and illustration geared to meet the changing needs of the fashion marketplace will find excitement, challenge, and profit in the various fashion areas. Because of the great diversity in this field, we will treat only some of the major areas here.

Department Stores

Most major department stores, in large metropolitan areas or in small towns, have art departments. In the smaller department stores, the art department may consist of an art director and a designer who will be responsible for designing advertisements that will run in the local newspapers. Large advertising departments in stores like Macy's or Bloomingdale's require a great number of designers and art directors, all responsible for various segments of fashion merchandise. For example, some of the large department stores may have a manager of window displays, whose primary function is to decorate the department store windows on a seasonal basis. Another designer or art director may be responsible for men's clothing, another for women's clothing, and perhaps another for fashion accessories and special projects. Major department stores do a tremendous amount of advertising on a daily basis, advertising products in virtually all areas of the fashion industry. The majority of the print advertising is black-and-white, since it will run in the local newspapers, but occasionally department stores will also use full-color television commercials as well as full-color advertising to be run in major newspaper supplements such as *Parade* magazine and the *New York Times Fashion Supplement*. Much of the color advertising will be put together by the advertising agency that handles the department store account. However, most of the black-and-white advertising will be done internally by the department store's art department.

Catalogs

Fashion catalogs display all the merchandise offered to the public and need extensive layout and design. Much of this work will be done internally by the department store advertising staff. There are special fashion catalog agencies that specialize in the development, execution, and production of department store catalogs, but catalog staff designers or art directors will do much of the planning and design. These catalogs usually are done in color and represent major promotions for the department stores.

Freelance Fashion Work

In addition to staff positions, department stores also offer excellent opportunities for freelance illustrators and photographers. Often a department store will maintain both a staff photographer and a staff illustrator to handle some of the more mundane newspaper advertising, particularly that which has to be done on a rush basis. For major advertisements, outside photographers and illustrators will be assigned particular illustrations and photographs, and these can pay very well for the freelancer. Frequently illustrators and photographers will be placed under a yearly contract that prevents them from working for any competitive department stores, although they can accept other kinds of freelance assignments.

In addition, outside photographers who specialize in catalog photography will be assigned to do catalog work under the direction of the department store art director. When doing catalogs, the illustrator or photographer will have to do a great many shots each day to meet the schedules of the department store catalog releases, particularly in conjunction with special sales.

The department store—and nearly every city or town has at least one—provides excellent opportunities for the artist who enjoys the world of fashion, either as a staff art director, designer, or layout artist, or as a freelance illustrator or photographer. The hours are long, and often the pay is low, but the excitement is always there.

Manufacturers and Wholesalers

A large part of the fashion business is made up of basic materials manufacturers who produce fabric and other materials related to the fashion industry, as well as wholesalers who will be supplying clothing, accessories, and other fashion materials to the department stores and other fashion-oriented retailers. These manufacturers and wholesalers do a tremendous amount of advertising to the trade and are an excellent source of work for the person interested in the fashion industry. Although the advertising may not be as creatively oriented as advertising done on the retail level, nevertheless, the manufacturing and wholesale fashion area can be exciting and lucrative for the art director, designer, or artist who enjoys this kind of work. Although opportunities for freelance illustration and photography are not as great as they are on the retail level (in many cases, staff artists or photographers will do most of the work), it is an area that should not be overlooked by freelancers.

In addition to all of the areas previously listed, the fashion industry provides tremendous opportunities for the freelance illustrator and photographer. Although the field is extremely competitive in nature, the successful illustrator or photographer specializing in the fashion area can make a good living while enjoying the exciting challenge of the incredible deadlines and changing moods of the fashion industry.

11

ARE YOU READY FOR THE REAL WORLD?

BEFORE YOU MAKE your decision about what kind of art school is right for you, or what part of the art field really appeals to you the most, you should take a realistic look at what these various art areas offer you. Just as in any other business—and the art field is just that—there are certain realities to be considered that may or may not make the field attractive to you.

For example, let's suppose you have made up your mind to be a freelance commercial graphic artist. That is really where your talent excels. You have the temperament, the talent, and the ambition. But what do you really know about the commercial art field and your chances of making a good living as a commercial artist in today's market?

No one really knows exactly how many visual artists there are in the business in the United States today, but according to government statistics, designers held about 492,000 jobs in the year 2000, and almost one-third of them were freelancers. It used to be that to be a designer, you had to live and work in the larger metropolitan areas like Boston, Chicago, Los Angeles, New York, and San Francisco. But great designers are now working all over the United States.

So, if your lifelong ambition is to live and work next to an old master illustrator while you carve out your own place in the world, take another look at these figures. That doesn't mean you shouldn't do it. It's just that you should be aware of the extent of the national competition that you will be facing every day.

New York isn't the only place in the country that buys commercial art. Most cities have at least one advertising agency, and consequently, even in small markets, many commercial artists are competing with one another for a piece of the artistic pie. Again, competition is one factor that can help make an artist a good artist. No one should or can live in a vacuum. But you should understand that the commercial users of art—the advertising agencies, the magazines, and the publishing houses—are not going to break down the door of your studio to give you that special job. You are going to have to go after that work, and that means you must become a salesperson as well as an artist.

You will want to ask yourself the following questions as you decide the direction of your career:

- Do you like showing work to strangers, not knowing what they think, or whether they will buy it?
- Do you like putting a price tag on your work and actually telling someone what you think your work is worth?
- Do you like knocking on doors and making cold calls to people at agencies or companies who may have absolutely no desire to see you at all? (After all, you called them; they didn't call you.)

- Can you stand the constant, day-in and day-out critiquing of you and your work, even though you know it is not meant to be intentionally cruel, but is done simply because your work is not what the client needs for that particular job at that particular time?

It is important to recognize that there are commercial artists who absolutely relish all of these challenges almost as much as they do illustrating the job. In fact, to many commercial artists, doing the job is only half the fun. But when you are candid with yourself, can you really accept this? Or would you much prefer sitting in your studio, solving artistic and design problems and letting someone else do the selling? Possibly at some point in your career, you can hire an agent to do that kind of work for you, but when you are starting out, no successful agent will be able to take you on as a talent because of your inexperience. At least in the beginning, you will be your own agent. You will be the person who is selling the work of an inexperienced artist.

How much money can you, as a commercial artist, make from year to year? That is a question you should at least think about before you commit yourself to years of art training.

According to *How Magazine*'s 2000 survey of salaries in graphic design, average salaries are up nearly 6 percent since 1998. Median annual salaries for graphic designers were $34,570 in 2000. The average entry-level designer made $30,775 in 2000. The average senior designer and Web designer earned $40,753, while the average art director made $53,127. Like the superstar movie actors who garner much of the publicity and the money, there are commercial artists in an artistic superstar category. These artists do the high-visibility advertising campaigns that everyone is talking about, or the string of popular paperback romances. These superstar commercial artists, like the superstar actors, are the exceptions. Most commercial artists work very hard to make even a small or modest income. The average freelance graphic designer reported median earnings of $50,000 in the year 2000. Artists making this kind of money can be and should be considered quite successful. It is very typical for a freelance artist to make more money annually than a salaried employee, but before you decide to go that route, you should weigh out the advantages and disadvantages of the freelance career.

So maybe being a freelance commercial artist doesn't appeal to you. Are you left to dangle off the edge of your board with no hope in sight? Of course not. You can become a salaried commercial artist. Upon graduation from art school—with your portfolio in hand—you will probably end up, quite realistically, on staff at an advertising agency, a publisher, or a promotion studio, doing felt marker comps or loose sketches based on someone else's ideas, or perhaps some storyboards. But this kind of job is a start. All agencies and studios need people like you, and you will be paid for it. You won't make a grand sum to start with, but at least you can earn a wage that will entitle you to call yourself a working illustrator. At some future date, you may want to become an art director or a designer. But for the time being, you will have a chance to learn your craft on the job. The competition, again, will be tough. There will be thousands of people out looking for exactly the same kind of salaried job as you want. But that's what makes the entire commercial art field so interesting.

Portfolios

If you are just beginning your studies, it is premature to talk about what goes into a selling portfolio or how to present a portfolio to a possible employer or client, but you will want to be developing the portfolio as you go along. It is important to point out that the artist portfolio is the most important thing you will ever use in your search for a job in all areas of the art field. The art school you choose to attend will show you how to put together a portfolio. That portfolio will change as you proceed through your artistic career. You will always be hired on the basis of your portfolio and your skills—and, in many cases, on the basis of your portfolio alone. Take your portfolio seriously. Learn all you can about what makes a good selling portfolio. Let the portfolio reflect your artistic and commercial personality. Portfolios evolve out of experience, but they are vital to your career at all stages of your artistic life.

Job Searches

Job searching is not only done using newspaper classified sections and cold calling anymore. Searching for design positions on the Internet has made job searching easier. General job search engines such as monster.com and hotjobs.com allow you to quickly find job openings in markets all over the United States. Specialized sites that search art and design jobs include creativehotlist.com and job-e-job.com.

You can also search sites that focus specifically on freelance design jobs, such as e-lance.com and freelancers.com. Most of these sites allow you to post your résumé and portfolio online so that companies can search for you as well!

Fine Artist Versus Reality

What about the fine artist who wants nothing to do with the commercial art scene and instead wants to paint or sculpt in the solitude of the studio? What are his or her chances of making a living in the art field as it exists today? These chances depend on what the artist is doing and who the agent is. The problems of being a fine artist are well documented in history. The ultimate impact of art on all civilization has always been made by fine artists making their unique personal statements in their work. A more "noble profession" could never be found, but in reality, it's a very tough way to make a living.

So, reality must be faced first if you are looking at the fine arts field as your ultimate goal. You will need to be cognizant of the pitfalls along the way to achieving that goal, which include the possibility of having to do something else while you experiment, polish, and improve your art. There is no easy shortcut to success in this aspect of the art field; but when you succeed, you can succeed in a very big way and the struggle will become that much more meaningful.

What About Art Direction?

In contemplating art direction as your area of interest, you should consider these facts:

- Every single advertising agency in the world, no matter how large or how small, needs the services of an art director. Not one print advertisement or television commercial, billboard, or brochure can be produced without the input and expertise of an art director.

- Not one magazine in the world can be "put to bed" without the design expertise—that is, the competence—of an art director overseeing the entire operation.

• Not one newspaper can ever find its way to any newsstand without one, two, three, or more art directors putting the thing together so it all makes sense.

Where Do You Fit In?

Where do you start fresh out of art school, with a portfolio to match your inexperience, in those advertising agencies, magazines, newspapers, and publishing companies? As in all other areas of your life, the economy has a great deal to do with where you start. It is amazing how many people in the art field at all levels think they live and work in a vacuum, unaffected by anything that happens around them, such as wars, recessions, and the like. But these things do affect everyone, sometimes in quite dramatic ways.

Suppose the economy is booming nationally and internationally. Manufacturers are spending money—lots of it—to gear up production to make more goods. The sales departments of these manufacturers are hiring more salespeople to hit the road and move the merchandise out. The advertising departments, and their advertising agencies, are gearing up for the yearlong advertising campaigns, and big money is going to be spent.

This is where you come in. When the economy is good and advertising dollars are being spent, there is a great need for new talent in all areas of the marketing mix. Advertising agencies will reactivate training programs for young potential art directors just out of art school. How long it will continue will depend on just how the economy fares.

Under ideal circumstances, the student coming out of art school with art director aspirations will be brought into a training program as an art director–trainee and will have the opportunity to work with full-fledged art directors on actual accounts and campaigns, in both print and television. The trainee will be able to learn the art direction business from the ground up. If there is no formal training program at the agency, the new graduate will be hired as an assistant art director. The assistant will likely be given little responsibility, but he or she will at least have a title and a presence within the agency, with work to accomplish and learn from. A student with the right portfolio has a chance to get in on the ground floor and start working. It can be done.

Appendix A

Professional Societies and Organizations

Advertising Photographers of America
145 S. Olive St.
Orange, CA 92866
apanational.org

Advertising Production Club of New York
60 E. Forty-Second St., Ste. 721
New York, NY 10165
apc-ny.org

Allied Artists of America
15 Gramercy Park South
New York, NY 10003
alliedartistsofamerica.org

American Association of Advertising Agencies
405 Lexington Ave., 18th Fl.
New York, NY 10174-1801
aaaa.org

American Film Institute
John F. Kennedy Center for the Performing Arts
2021 N. Western Ave.
Los Angeles, CA 90027
afi.com

American Institute of Graphic Arts
164 Fifth Ave.
New York, NY 10010
aiga.org

American Society of Media Photographers
150 N. Second St.
Philadelphia, PA 19106
asmp.org

Art Directors Club of New York
106 W. Twenty-Ninth St.
New York, NY 10001
adcny.org

Association for Graphic Arts Training
2501 Powell Ave.
Nashville, TN 37204
agatweb.org

Association of Graphic Communication
330 Seventh Ave., Ninth Fl.
New York, NY 10001
agcomm.org

Association of Internet Professionals
866-AIP-9700
association.org

The Association of Medical Illustrators
5475 Mark Dabling Blvd., Ste. 108
Colorado Springs, CO 80918
ami.org

Chicago Art Dealers Association
730 N. Franklin, Ste. 004
Chicago, IL 60610
artline.com

Color Association of the United States
315 W. Thirty-Ninth St., Studio 507
New York, NY 10018
colorassociation.com

Color Marketing Group
5904 Richmond Highway, No. 408
Alexandria, VA 22303
colormarketing.org

Design Management Institute
29 Temple Pl., 2nd Fl.
Boston, MA 02111
dmi.org

Digital Printing and Imaging Association
10015 Main St.
Fairfax, VA 22031-3489
dpia.org

Graphic Artists Guild
90 John St., Ste. 403
New York, NY 10011
gag.org

Graphic Communications Association
100 Daingerfield Rd., 4th Fl.
Alexandria, VA 22314-2888
idealliance.org

Greeting Card Association
1156 Fifteenth St. NW, Ste. 900
Washington, DC 20005
greetingcard.org

Guild of Natural Science Illustrators
P.O. Box 652
Ben Franklin Station
Washington, DC 20044-0652
gnsi.org

International Association of Webmasters and Designers
13833-E4 Wellington Trace, PMB, Ste. #214
Wellington, FL 33414
iawmd.org

International Game Developers Network
600 Harrison
San Francisco, CA 94107
igdn.org

National Association of Schools of Art and Design
11250 Roger Bacon Dr., Ste. 21
Reston, VA 22090
arts-accredit.org

Society for Environmental Graphic Design
401 F St. NW, Ste. 333
Washington, DC 20001-2728
segd.org

Society of Illustrators
128 E. Sixty-Third St.
New York, NY 10021
societyillustrators.org

Society for News Design
1130 Ten Rod Rd., Ste. F-104
North Kingstown, RI 02852
snd.org

Society of Publication Designers
60 E. Forty-Second St., Ste. 721
New York, NY 10165
spd.org

Urban Art International
P.O. Box 868
Tiburon, CA 94920
imagesite.com

Western Art Directors Club
P.O. Box 996
Palo Alto, CA 94302
wadc.org

Women in Production
276 Bowery
New York, NY 10012
wip.org

Appendix B

Periodicals

Advertising Age
Crain Communications, Inc.
740 Rush St.
Chicago, IL 60611-2590
aamedia.chaffee.com

Adweek
BPI Communications
770 Broadway
New York, NY 10003
adweek.com

American Artist
BPI Communications
770 Broadway
New York, NY 10003
myamericanartist.com

American Printer
Primedia Business Magazines
29 N. Wacker Dr.
Chicago, IL 60606-3298
americanprinter.com

Architecture
BPI Communications
770 Broadway
New York, NY 10003
architecturemag.com

Art in America
artinamericamagazine.com

ARTnews
48 W. Thirty-Eighth St.
New York, NY 10018-6211
artnews.com

BrandWeek
BPI Communications
770 Broadway
New York, NY 10003
brandweek.com

Communication Arts
110 Constitution Dr.
Menlo Park, CA 94025
commarts.com

Computer Graphics World
PennWell Publishing Co.
98 Spit Brook Rd.
Nashua, NH 03062-2800
cgw.pennet.com

Design and Display Ideas
BPI Communications
770 Broadway
New York, NY 10003
ddimagazine.com

Design News
Reed Business Publications
360 Park Ave. South
New York, NY 10010
manufacturing.net/dn

Graphic Arts Monthly
Reed Business Publications
360 Park Ave. South
New York, NY 10010
gammag.com

Graphic Design: USA
79 Madison Ave., Ste. 1202
New York, NY 10016
gdusa.com

Graphis
307 Fifth Ave., 10th Fl.
New York, NY 10016
graphis.com

Greetings, Etc.
Edgell Communications, Inc.
4 Middlebury Blvd.
Randolph, NJ 07869
greetingsmagazine.com

How Magazine
F&W Publications, Inc.
4700 E. Galbraith Rd.
Cincinnati, OH 45236
howdesign.com

ID: Magazine of International Design
idonline.com

PDN (Photo District News)
BPI Communications
770 Broadway
New York, NY 10003
pdnonline.com

Print
printmag.com

Publishers Weekly
Reed Business Publications
360 Park Ave. South
New York, NY 10010
publishersweekly.com

Trendwatch Graphic Arts
Reed Business Publications
360 Park Ave. South
New York, NY 10010
trendwatchgraphicarts.com

Appendix C

Training Programs/Schools

THE FOLLOWING SCHOOLS offer degree programs in the graphic arts. Schools marked with an asterisk (*) are accredited by the National Association of Schools of Art and Design.

Alabama

Auburn University*
Auburn, AL 36849
auburn.edu

Birmingham-Southern College
Birmingham, AL 35254
bsc.edu

Jacksonville State University*
Jacksonville, AL 36265
jsucc.edu

Samford University
   Birmingham, AL 35229
   samford.edu

University of Alabama at Birmingham*
   Birmingham, AL 35294
   uab.edu

University of Alabama at Tuscaloosa*
   Tuscaloosa, AL 35847
   ua.edu

University of Montevallo*
   Montevallo, AL 35115
   montevallo.edu

University of North Alabama*
   Florence, AL 35632
   una.edu

University of South Alabama*
   Mobile, AL 36688
   southalabama.edu

Alaska

University of Alaska, Anchorage*
   Anchorage, AK 99508
   uaa.alaska.edu

Arizona

Arizona State University*
   Tempe, AZ 85287
   asu.edu

The Art Institute of Phoenix
Phoenix, AZ 85021
aipx.edu

Grand Canyon University
Phoenix, AZ 85017
grand-canyon.edu

Northern Arizona University
Flagstaff, AZ 86011
nau.edu

University of Arizona*
Tucson, AZ 85721
arizona.edu

Arkansas

Arkansas State University*
State University, AR 72467
astate.edu

John Brown University
Siloam Springs, AR 72761
jbu.edu

University of Arkansas at Little Rock*
Little Rock, AR 72204
ualr.edu

California

Academy of Art College*
San Francisco, CA 94105
academyart.edu

Art Center College of Design*
Pasadena, CA 91103
artcenter.edu

Art Institute of California–Los Angeles
Santa Monica, CA 90405
aicala.artinstitutes.edu

Art Institute of California–San Diego
San Diego, CA 92122
taac.edu

Art Institute of California–San Francisco
San Francisco, CA 94102
aisf.aii.edu

Art Institute of Southern California
Laguna Beach, CA 92651
aisc.edu

California College of Arts and Crafts*
San Francisco, CA 94107
ccac-art.edu

California Institute of the Arts*
Valencia, CA 91355
calarts.edu

California Polytechnic State University, Pomona
Pomona, CA 91768
csupomona.edu

California Polytechnic State University, San Luis Obispo
San Luis Obispo, CA 93407
calpoly.edu

California State University, Chico*
Chico, CA 95929
csuchico.edu

California State University, Dominguez Hills
Carson, CA 90747
csudh.edu

California State University, Fullerton*
Fullerton, CA 92834
fullerton.edu

California State University, Hayward*
Hayward, CA 94542
csuhayward.edu

California State University, Long Beach*
Long Beach, CA 90840
csulb.edu

California State University, Los Angeles*
Los Angeles, CA 90032
calstatela.edu

California State University, Northridge*
Northridge, CA 91330
csun.edu

California State University, Sacramento*
Sacramento, CA 95819
csus.edu

California State University, San Bernardino*
San Bernardino, CA 92407
csusb.edu

California State University, Stanislaus*
Turlock, CA 95382
csustan.edu

Chapman University
Orange, CA 92866
chapman.edu

Cogswell Polytechnical College
Sunnyvale, CA 94089
cogswell.edu

College of Notre Dame
Belmont, CA 94002
ndnu.edu

Humboldt State University*
Arcata, CA 95521
humboldt.edu

La Sierra University
Riverside, CA 92515
lasierra.edu

Loyola Marymount University*
Los Angeles, CA 90045
lmu.edu

Newschool of Architecture and Design
San Diego, CA 92101
newschoolarch.edu

Otis College of Art and Design*
Los Angeles, CA 90045
otis.edu

Platt College
  Newport Beach, CA 92660
  plattcollege.edu

Point Loma Nazarene College
  San Diego, CA 92106
  ptloma.edu

San Diego State University*
  San Diego, CA 92182
  sdsu.edu

San Francisco Art Institute*
  San Francisco, CA 94133
  sfai.edu

San Jose State University*
  San Jose, CA 95192
  sjsu.edu

Sonoma State University*
  Rohnert Park, CA 94928
  sonoma.edu

University of California–Davis
  Davis, CA 95616
  ucdavis.edu

University of the Pacific*
  Stockton, CA 95211
  pacific.edu

University of San Francisco
  San Francisco, CA 94117
  usfca.edu

Woodbury University
Burbank, CA 91510
woodbury.edu

Colorado

The Art Institute of Colorado
Denver, CO 80203
aic.aii.edu

Colorado State University
Ft. Collins, CO 80523
colostate.edu

Platt College
Aurora, CO 80014
plattcolo.com

Rocky Mountain College of Arts and Design
Denver, CO 80224
rmcad.edu

University of Denver*
Denver, CO 80208
du.edu

University of Northern Colorado
Greeley, CO 80639
unco.edu

Connecticut

Central Connecticut State University
New Britain, CT 06050
ccsu.edu

Lyme Academy of Fine Arts*
Old Lyme, CT 06371
lymeacademy.edu

Paier College of Art
Hamden, CT 06514
paierart.com

Sacred Heart University
Fairfield, CT 06825
sacredheart.edu

Southern Connecticut State University
New Haven, CT 06515
southernct.edu

University of Bridgeport*
Bridgeport, CT 06601
bridgeport.edu

University of Connecticut*
Storrs, CT 06269
uconn.edu

University of Hartford
West Hartford, CT 06117
hartford.edu

University of New Haven
West Haven, CT 06516
newhaven.edu

Western Connecticut State University
Danbury, CT 06810
wcsu.edu

Yale University
New Haven, CT 06520
yale.edu

Delaware

University of Delaware
Newark, DE 19716
udel.edu

District of Columbia

American University
Washington, DC 20016
american.edu

The Corcoran College of Art and Design*
Washington, DC 20006
corcoran.org

Gallaudet University
Washington, DC 20002
gallaudet.edu

Howard University*
Washington, DC 20059
howard.edu

Florida

Art Institute of Fort Lauderdale
Fort Lauderdale, FL 33316
aifl.edu

Flagler College
St. Augustine, FL 32085
flagler.edu

Florida A&M University
Tallahassee, FL 32307
famu.edu

Florida State University*
Tallahassee, FL 32306
fsu.edu

International Academy of Design and Technology
Tampa, FL 33634
academy.edu

Lynn University
Boca Raton, FL 33431
lynn.edu

Ringling School of Art and Design*
Sarasota, FL 34234
rsad.edu

University of Central Florida
Orlando, FL 32816
ucf.edu

University of Florida*
Gainesville, FL 32611
ufl.edu

University of Miami
Coral Gables, FL 33146
miami.edu

University of North Florida
   Jacksonville, FL 32224
   unf.edu

Georgia

Art Institute of Atlanta
   Atlanta, GA 30328
   aia.aii.edu

Atlanta College of Art*
   Atlanta, GA 30309
   aca.edu

Georgia Southwestern State University
   Americus, GA 31709
   gsw.edu

Georgia State University*
   Atlanta, GA 30303
   gsu.edu

Savannah College of Art and Design
   Savannah, GA 31402
   scad.edu

University of Georgia*
   Athens, GA 30602
   uga.edu

Valdosta State University*
   Valdosta, GA 31698
   valdosta.edu

Illinois

Bradley University*
Peoria, IL 61625
bradley.edu

Chicago State University
Chicago, IL 60628
csu.edu

Columbia College
Chicago, IL 60605
colum.edu

DePaul University
Chicago, IL 60604
depaul.edu

Eastern Illinois University*
Charleston, IL 61920
eiu.edu

Illinois State University*
Normal, IL 61790
ilstu.edu

Illinois Wesleyan University
Bloomington, IL 61702
iwu.edu

Judson College
Elgin, IL 60123
judson-il.edu

North Central College
Naperville, IL 60540
northcentralcollege.edu

Northern Illinois University*
De Kalb, IL 60113
niu.edu

Northwestern University
Evanston, IL 60204
northwestern.edu

Olivet Nazarene University
Bourbonnais, IL 60914
olivet.edu

Saint Xavier University
Chicago, IL 60655
sxu.edu

School of the Art Institute of Chicago*
Chicago, IL 60603
artic.edu

Southern Illinois University at Carbondale*
Carbondale, IL 62901
siuc.edu

University of Illinois at Chicago*
Chicago, IL 60680
uic.edu

University of Illinois at Urbana-Champaign*
Urbana, IL 61801
uiuc.edu

Indiana

Anderson University
Anderson, IN 46012
anderson.edu

Ball State University*
Muncie, IN 47306
bsu.edu

Grace College
Winona Lake, IN 46590
grace.edu

Huntington College
Huntington, IN 46750
huntington.edu

Indiana State University*
Terre Haute, IN 47809
indstate.edu

Indiana University*
Bloomington, IN 47405
indiana.edu

Indiana University—Purdue University Indianapolis
Indianapolis, IN 46202
iupui.edu

Purdue University
West Lafayette, IN 47907
purdue.edu

Saint Mary's College*
Notre Dame, IN 46556
saintmarys.edu

Taylor University
Upland, IN 46989
tayloru.edu

University of Evansville
Evansville, IN 47722
evansville.edu

Vincennes University*
Vincennes, IN 47591
vinu.edu

Iowa

Drake University*
Des Moines, IA 50311
choose.drake.edu

Iowa State University of Science and Technology
Ames, IA 50011
iastate.edu

Morningside College
Sioux City, IA 51106
morningside.edu

St. Ambrose University
Davenport, IA 52803
sau.edu

University of Iowa
Iowa City, IA 52242
uiowa.edu

University of Northern Iowa*
Cedar Falls, IA 50614
uni.edu

Upper Iowa University
Fayette, IA 52142
uiu.edu

Kansas

Fort Hays State University
Hays, KS 67601
fhsu.edu

Pittsburg State University
Pittsburg, KS 66762
pittstate.edu

University of Kansas*
Lawrence, KS 66045
ku.edu

Washburn University of Topeka*
Topeka, KS 66621
washburn.edu

Wichita State University
Wichita, KS 67260
wichita.edu

Kentucky

Brescia College
Owensboro, KY 42301
brescia.edu

Eastern Kentucky University
Richmond, KY 40475
eku.edu

Murray State University*
Murray, KY 42071
murraystate.edu

Northern Kentucky University
Highland Heights, KY 41099
nku.edu

Western Kentucky University*
Bowling Green, KY 42101
wku.edu

Louisiana

Louisiana State University and Agricultural and Mechanical College*
Baton Rouge, LA 70803
lsu.edu

Louisiana Tech University*
Ruston, LA 71272
latech.edu

Loyola University, New Orleans
New Orleans, LA 70118
loyno.edu

Northwestern State University of Louisiana
Natchitoches, LA 71497
nsula.edu

University of New Orleans*
New Orleans, LA 70148
uno.edu

Maine

Maine College of Art*
Portland, ME 04101
meca.edu

New England School of Communications
Bangor, ME 04401
nescom.edu

University of Southern Maine*
Gorham, ME 04038
maine.edu

Maryland

College of Notre Dame of Maryland
Baltimore, MD 21210
ndm.edu

Frostburg State University
Frostburg, MD 21532
frostburg.edu

Hood College
Frederick, MD 21701
hood.edu

Maryland College of Art and Design*
Silver Spring, MD 20902
mcadmd.org

Maryland Institute, College of Art*
Baltimore, MD 21217
mica.edu

McDaniel College
Westminster, MD 21157
mcdaniel.edu

Salisbury University
Salisbury, MD 21801
salisbury.edu

Massachusetts

Art Institute of Boston*
Boston, MA 02215
aiboston.edu

Boston University
Boston, MA 02215
bu.edu

Bridgewater State College
  Bridgewater, MA 02325
  bridgew.edu

Clark University
  Worcester, MA 01610
  clarku.edu

Curry College
  Milton, MA 02186
  curry.edu

Emerson College
  Boston, MA 02116
  emerson.edu

Emmanuel College
  Boston, MA 02115
  emmanuel.edu

Endicott College
  Beverly, MA 01915
  endicott.edu

Fitchburg State College
  Fitchburg, MA 01420
  fsc.edu

Hampshire College
  Amherst, MA 01002
  hampshire.edu

Massachusetts College of Art*
  Boston, MA 02115
  massart.edu

Montserrat College of Art*
Beverly, MA 01915
montserrat.edu

Mount Ida College*
Newton Centre, MA 02459
mountida.edu

The New England Institute of Art and Communication
Brookline, MA 02445
aine.artinstitute.edu

Salem State College*
Salem, MA 01970
salemstate.edu

School of the Museum of Fine Arts*
Boston, MA 02115
smfa.edu

Simmons College
Boston, MA 02115
simmons.edu

Suffolk University
Boston, MA 02108
suffolk.edu

University of Massachusetts–Dartmouth*
North Dartmouth, MA 02747
umassd.edu

University of Massachusetts–Lowell*
Lowell, MA 01854
uml.edu

Westfield State College
Westfield, MA 01086
wsc.mass.edu

Michigan

Andrews University
Berrien Springs, MI 49104
andrews.edu

Aquinas College
Grand Rapids, MI 49506
aquinas.edu

Baker College of Flint
Flint, MI 48507
baker.edu

Baker College of Owosso
Owosso, MI 48867
owosso.baker.edu

Central Michigan University
Mount Pleasant, MI 48859
cmich.edu

College for Creative Studies—College of Art and Design*
Detroit, MI 48202
ccscad.edu

Cranbrook Academy of Art*
Bloomfield Hills, MI 48303
cranbrookart.edu

Eastern Michigan University
Ypsilanti, MI 48197
emich.edu

Grand Valley State University*
Allendale, MI 49401
gvsu.edu

Hope College*
Holland, MI 49422
hope.edu

Kendall College of Art and Design*
Grand Rapids, MI 49503
kcad.edu

Madonna University
Livonia, MI 48150
munet.edu

Michigan State University
East Lansing, MI 48823
msu.edu

Northern Michigan University
Marquette, MI 49855
nmu.edu

Saginaw Valley State University
University Center, MI 48710
svsu.edu

Siena Heights College*
Adrian, MI 49221
sienahts.edu

University of Michigan*
Ann Arbor, MI 48128
umich.edu

Wayne State University
Detroit, MI 48202
wayne.edu

Western Michigan University*
Kalamazoo, MI 49008
wmich.edu

Minnesota

Bemidji State University
Bemidji, MN 56601
bemidjistate.edu

College of Visual Arts
St. Paul, MN 55102
cva.edu

Minneapolis College of Art and Design*
Minneapolis, MN 55404
mcad.edu

Minnesota State University, Mankato*
Mankato, MN 56002
mnsu.edu

Minnesota State University, Moorhead*
Moorhead, MN 56563
mnstate.edu

Northwestern College
St. Paul, MN 55113
nwc.edu

Saint Mary's University of Minnesota
Winona, MN 55987
smumn.edu

St. Cloud State University*
St. Cloud, MN 56301
stcloudstate.edu

University of Minnesota–Duluth
Duluth, MN 55812
umn.edu

Winona State University
Winona, MN 55987
winona.edu

Mississippi

Belhaven College*
Jackson, MS 39202
bellhaven.edu

Delta State University*
Cleveland, MS 38733
deltast.edu

Jackson State University*
Jackson, MS 39217
jsums.edu

Mississippi State University*
Mississippi State, MS 39762
msstate.edu

Mississippi University for Women*
Columbus, MS 39701
muw.edu

Mississippi Valley State University*
Itta Bena, MS 38941
mvsu.edu

University of Mississippi*
University, MS 38677
olemiss.edu

University of Southern Mississippi*
Hattiesburg, MS 39406
usm.edu

Missouri

Central Missouri State University*
Warrensburg, MO 64093
cmsu.edu

College of the Ozarks
Point Lookout, MO 65726
cofo.edu

Columbia College
Columbia, MO 65216
ccis.edu

Kansas City Art Institute*
Kansas City, MO 64111
kcai.edu

Maryville University of Saint Louis*
St. Louis, MO 63141
maryville.edu

Northwest Missouri State University
Maryville, MO 64468
nwmissouri.edu

Park College
Parkville, MO 64152
park.edu

Southwest Missouri State University
Springfield, MO 65804
smsu.edu

St. Louis Community College at Florrisant Valley*
St. Louis, MO 63135
stlcc.mo.us/fv

University of Missouri–Columbia
Columbia, MO 65211
missouri.edu

Washington University*
St. Louis, MO 63130
wustl.edu

Webster University
St. Louis, MO 63119
webster.edu

Westminster College
Fulton, MO 65251
westminster-mo.edu

William Woods University
Fulton, MO 65251
williamwoods.edu

Montana

Montana State University–Billings*
Billings, MT 59101
msubillings.edu

Montana State University–Bozeman*
Bozeman, MT 59717
montana.edu

Montana State University–Northern
Havre, MT 59501
nmclites.edu

The University of Montana–Missoula*
Missoula, MT 59812
umt.edu

Nebraska

Creighton University
Omaha, NE 68178
creighton.edu

Dana College
Blair, NE 68008
dana.edu

University of Nebraska–Lincoln*
Lincoln, NE 68588
unl.edu

Wayne State College
Wayne, NE 68787
wsc.edu

Nevada

University of Nevada–Las Vegas*
Las Vegas, NV 89154
unlv.edu

New Hampshire

Colby-Sawyer College
New London, NH 03257
colby-sawyer.edu

Franklin Pierce College
Rindge, NH 03461
fpc.edu

Keene State University
Keene, NH 03435
keene.edu

New England College
Henniker, NH 03242
nec.edu

New Hampshire Institute of Art*
Manchester, NH 03104
nhia.edu

Plymouth State College
Plymouth, NH 03264
plymouth.edu

Rivier College
Nashua, NH 03060
rivier.edu

New Jersey

Bloomfield College
Bloomfield, NJ 07003
bloomfield.edu

Centenary College
Hackettstown, NJ 07840
centenarycollege.edu

Fairleigh Dickinson University
Teaneck, NJ 07666
fdu.edu

Felician College
Lodi, NJ 07644
felician.edu

Kean University*
Union, NJ 07083
kean.edu

Montclair State University*
Upper Montclair, NJ 07043
montclair.edu

New Jersey City University*
Jersey City, NJ 07305
njcu.edu

Rowan University*
Glassboro, NJ 08028
rowan.edu

Rutgers, The State University of New Jersey
New Brunswick, NJ 08903
rutgers.edu

The College of New Jersey
Ewing, NJ 08628
tcnj.edu

William Paterson College of New Jersey
Wayne, NJ 07470
ww2.wpunj.edu

New Mexico

Eastern New Mexico University
Portales, NM 88130
enmu.edu

Institute of American Indian Arts*
Santa Fe, NM 85508
iaiancad.org

New Mexico Highlands University
Las Vegas, NM 87701
nmnu.edu

New York

Alfred University*
Alfred, NY 14802
alfred.edu

Cazenovia College
Cazenovia, NY 13035
cazenovia.edu

College of Saint Rose*
Albany, NY 12203
strose.edu

Cooper Union for the Advancement of Science and Art*
New York, NY 10003
cooper.edu

Cornell University
Ithaca, NY 14850
cornell.edu

Daemen College
Amherst, NY 14226
daemen.edu

Fashion Institute of Technology*
New York, NY 10001
fitny.edu

Fordham University
New York, NY 10458
fordham.edu

Hartwick College*
    Oneonta, NY 13820
    hartwick.edu

Long Island University, CW Post Campus
    Brookville, NY 11548
    liu.edu

Long Island University, Southampton Campus
    Southampton, NY 11968
    southampton.liu.edu

Mercy College
    Dobbs Ferry, NY 10522
    mercy.edu

New York City Technical College of the City University of New York
    Brooklyn, NY 11201
    nyctc.cuny.edu

New York Institute of Technology
    Old Westbury, NY 11568
    nyit.edu

New York University
    New York, NY 10011
    nyu.edu

Parsons School of Design*
    New York, NY 10011
    parsons.edu

Pratt Institute*
Brooklyn, NY 11205
pratt.edu

Roberts Wesleyan College*
Rochester, NY 14624
roberts.edu

Rochester Institute of Technology*
Rochester, NY 14623
rit.edu

Sage College of Albany*
Albany, NY 12208
sage.edu

School of Visual Arts*
New York, NY 10010
schoolofvisualarts.edu

Skidmore College*
Saratoga Springs, NY 12866
skidmore.edu

St. John's University
Jamaica, NY 11439
stjohns.edu

State University of New York at Buffalo
Buffalo, NY 14222
buffalostate.edu

State University of New York at New Paltz*
New Paltz, NY 12561
newpaltz.edu

Syracuse University*
    Syracuse, NY 13244
    syracuse.edu

North Carolina

Appalachian State University*
    Boone, NC 28608
    appstate.edu

Barton College
    Wilson, NC 27893
    barton.edu

Campbell University
    Buies Creek, NC 27506
    campbell.edu

Chowan College
    Murfreesboro, NC 27855
    chowan.edu

East Carolina State University*
    Greenville, NC 27858
    ecu.edu

Meredith College
    Raleigh, NC 27607
    meredith.edu

North Carolina State University
    Raleigh, NC 27695
    ncsu.edu

North Dakota

University of North Dakota*
Grand Forks, ND 58202
und.edu

Ohio

Art Academy of Cincinnati*
Cincinnati, OH 45202
artacademy.edu

Bowling Green State University*
Bowling Green, OH 43402
bgsu.edu

Central State University
Wilberforce, OH 45384
centralstate.edu

Cleveland Institute of Art*
Cleveland, OH 44106
cia.edu

College of Mount St. Joseph
Cincinnati, OH 45233
msj.edu

Columbus College of Art and Design*
Columbus, OH 43215
ccad.edu

Kent State University*
Kent, OH 44242
kent.edu

Miami University of Ohio*
Oxford, OH 45056
muohio.edu

Ohio Northern University
Ada, OH 45810
ohu.edu

Ohio State University*
Columbus, OH 43210
osu.edu

Ohio University
Athens, OH 45701
ohiou.edu

University of Akron*
Akron, OH 44325
akron.edu

University of Cincinnati*
Cincinnati, OH 45221
uc.edu

University of Dayton
Dayton, OH 45469
udayton.edu

Wittenberg University
Springfield, OH 45501
wittenberg.edu

Xavier University
Cincinnati, OH 45207
xavier.edu

Youngstown State University*
Youngstown, OH 44555
ysu.edu

Oklahoma

Northeastern State University
Tahlequah, OK 74464
nsuok.edu

Oklahoma State University
Stillwater, OK 74078
okstate.edu

University of Central Oklahoma
Edmond, OK 73034
ucok.edu

Oregon

Art Institute of Portland
Portland, OR 97201
aipd.artinstitute.edu

Oregon School of Arts and Crafts*
Portland, OR 97225
ocac.edu

Pacific Northwest College of Art*
Portland, OR 97209
pnca.edu

Portland State University*
Portland, OR 97207
pdx.edu

University of Oregon
Eugene, OR 97403
uoregon.edu

Western Oregon University
Monmouth, OR 97361
wou.edu

Pennsylvania

Arcadia College*
Glenside, PA 19038
arcadia.edu

Art Institute of Philadelphia
Philadelphia, PA 19103
aiph.aii.edu

Art Institute of Pittsburgh
Pittsburgh, PA 15222
aip.aii.edu

Bradley Academy for the Visual Arts
York, PA 17402
bradleyacademy.edu

Bucks County Community College*
Newtown, PA 18940
bucks.edu

California University of Pennsylvania
California, PA 15419
cup.edu

Carnegie Mellon University*
Pittsburgh, PA 15213
cmu.edu

Cedar Crest College
Allentown, PA 18104
cedarcrest.edu

Drexel University
Philadelphia, PA 19104
drexel.edu

Edinboro University of Pennsylvania
Edinboro, PA 16444
edinboro.edu

Hussian School of Art
Philadelphia, PA 19107
hussianart.edu

La Roche College*
Pittsburgh, PA 15237
laroche.edu

Lycoming Hill
Williamsport, PA 17701
lycoming.edu

Marywood University*
Scranton, PA 18509
marywood.edu

Mercyhurst College
Erie, PA 16546
mercyhurst.edu

Millersville University of Pennsylvania
Millersville, PA 17551
millersville.edu

Moore College of Art and Design*
Philadelphia, PA 19103
moore.edu

Moravian College
Bethlehem, PA 18018
moravian.edu

Oakbridge Academy of Art
Lower Burrell, PA 15068
oakbridgeacademy.com

Pennsylvania Academy of the Fine Arts*
Philadelphia, PA 19107
pafa.org

Pennsylvania College of Technology
Williamsport, PA 17701
pct.edu

Pennsylvania School of Art and Design
Lancaster, PA 17608
psad.edu

Pennsylvania State University*
University Park, PA 16804
psu.edu

Philadelphia University
Philadelphia, PA 19144
philau.edu

Saint Vincent College
  Latrobe, PA 15650
  stvincent.edu

Seton Hill College
  Greensburg, PA 15601
  setonhill.edu

Temple University
  Philadelphia, PA 19122
  temple.edu

University of the Arts*
  Philadelphia, PA 19102
  uarts.edu

Rhode Island

Rhode Island College*
  Providence, RI 02908
  ric.edu

Rhode Island School of Design*
  Providence, RI 02905
  risd.edu

Salve Regina University*
  Newport, RI 02840
  salve.edu

South Carolina

Anderson College
  Anderson, SC 29621
  ac.edu

Clemson University*
  Clemson, SC 29634
  clemson.edu

Coker College
  Hartsville, SC 29550
  coker.edu

Columbia College*
  Columbia, SC 29203
  columbiacollegesc.edu

University of South Carolina*
  Columbia, SC 29208
  sc.edu

Winthrop University*
  Rock Hill, SC 29733
  winthrop.edu

South Dakota

Black Hills State University
  Spearfish, SD 57799
  bhsu.edu

University of South Dakota*
  Vermilion, SD 57069
  usd.edu

Tennessee

Austin Peay State University*
  Clarksville, TN 37044
  apsu.edu

Belmont University
Nashville, TN 37212
belmont.edu

Carson-Newman College*
Jefferson City, TN 37760
cn.edu

East Tennessee State University*
Johnson City, TN 37614
etsu.edu

Freed-Hardeman University
Henderson, TN 38340
fhu.edu

Memphis College of Art*
Memphis, TN 38104
mca.edu

Middle Tennessee State University
Murfreesboro, TN 37132
mtsu.edu

Nossi College of Art
Goodlettsville, TN 37022
nossi.edu

O'More College of Design
Franklin, TN 37064
omorecollege.edu

The University of Memphis*
Memphis, TN 38152
memphis.edu

University of Tennessee–Chattanooga*
Chattanooga, TN 37403
utc.edu

University of Tennessee–Knoxville*
Knoxville, TN 37996
tennessee.edu

Texas

Abilene Christian University
Abilene, TX 79699
acu.edu

Art Institute of Dallas
Dallas, TX 75231
aid.artinstitute.edu

The Art Institute of Houston
Houston, TX 77056
aih.aii.edu

Del Mar College*
Corpus Christi, TX 78404
delmar.edu

Lamar University–Beaumont
Beaumont, TX 77710
lamar.edu

Lubbock Christian University
Lubbock, TX 79407
lcu.edu

Texas Tech University*
Lubbock, TX 79409
ttu.edu

University of Houston
Houston, TX 77204
uh.edu

University of North Texas
Denton, TX 76203
unt.edu

University of Texas at El Paso
El Paso, TX 79968
utep.edu

University of Texas at San Antonio*
San Antonio, TX 78249
utsa.edu

West Texas A&M University
Canyon, TX 79016
wtmau.edu

Utah

Brigham Young University*
Provo, UT 84602
byu.edu

Weber State University
Ogden, UT 84408
weber.edu

Vermont

Lyndon State College
Lyndonville, VT 05851
lyndonstate.edu

Virginia

Art Institute of Washington
Arlington, VA 22209
aiw.artinstitute.edu

Hampton University
Hampton, VA 23668
hamptonu.edu

James Madison University*
Harrisonburg, VA 22807
jmu.edu

Liberty University
Lynchburg, VA 24502
liberty.edu

Longwood College
Farmville, VA 23909
longwood.edu

Mary Baldwin College
Staunton, VA 24401
mbc.edu

Marymount University
Arlington, VA 22207
marymount.edu

Radford University
Radford, VA 24142
radford.edu

Virginia Commonwealth University*
Richmond, VA 23284
vcu.edu

Washington

Art Institute of Seattle
Seattle, WA 98122
ais.edu

Central Washington University
Ellensburg, WA 98926
cwu.edu

Cornish College of the Arts*
Seattle, WA 98102
cornish.edu

Heritage College
Toppenish, WA 98948
heritage.edu

Northwest College of Art
Poulsbo, WA 98370
nca.edu

University of Washington
Seattle, WA 98195
uwashington.edu

Walla Walla College
College Place, WA 99324
wwc.edu

West Virginia

Fairmont State College
Fairmont, WV 26554
fscwv.edu

Marshall University
Huntington, WV 25755
marshall.edu

Shepherd College
Shepherdstown, WV 25443
shepherd.edu

West Liberty State College
West Liberty, WV 26074
wlsc.edu

West Virginia University*
Morgantown, WV 26506
wvu.edu

West Virginia Wesleyan College
Buckhannon, WV 26201
wvwc.edu

Wisconsin

Carthage College
Kenosha, WI 53140
carthage.edu

Concordia University
Mequon, WI 53097
cuw.edu

Edgewood College
Madison, WI 53713
edgewood.edu

Milwaukee Institute of Art and Design*
Milwaukee, WI 53202
miad.edu

Mount Mary College
Milwaukee, WI 53222
mtmary.edu

St. Norbert College
De Pere, WI 54115
snc.edu

University of Wisconsin–Madison*
Madison, WI 53706
wisc.edu

University of Wisconsin–Platteville
Platteville, WI 53818
uwplatt.edu

University of Wisconsin–Stevens Point*
Stevens Point, WI 54481
uwsp.edu

University of Wisconsin–Stout*
Menomonie, WI 54751
uwstout.edu

BIBLIOGRAPHY

Arntson, Amy. *Graphic Design Basics*. 4th ed. Belmont, Calif.: Wadsworth Publishing Company, 2002.

Aynsley, Jeremy. *A Century of Graphic Design*. Hauppauge, N.Y.: Barron's Educational Series, Inc., 2001.

Bates, Bob. *Game Design: The Art and Business of Creating Games*. Premier Press, 2002.

Benun, Ilise. *Designing Web Sites for Every Audience*. How Design Books, 2003.

Blount, Tricia. *Film and Television 2000: Production Makers Source of the Madison Avenue Handbook*. Peter Glenn Publications, 2000.

Bowen, Linda Cooper. *The Graphic Designers Guide to Creative Marketing: Finding and Keeping Your Best Clients*. Hoboken, N.J.: John Wiley & Sons, 1999.

Campbell, Alastair. *The Designer's Lexicon: The Illustrated Dictionary of Design, Printing and Computer Terms*. San Francisco: Chronicle Books, 2000.

Carson, David, and Lewis Blackwell. *The End of Print*. Rev. ed. San Francisco: Chronicle Books, 2000.

Cohen, Luanne Seymour. *Design Essentials for Adobe Photoshop 7 and Illustrator 10*. 4th ed. Adobe Press, 2002.

Cox, Mary. *2003 Artist's and Graphic Designer's Market: 2,100+ Places to Sell Your Illustrations, Fine Art, Graphic Designs and Cartoons*. Cincinnati: Writer's Digest Books, 2002. (Annual)

Crawford, Tad, and Eva D. Bruck. *Business & Legal Forms for Graphic Designers*. New York: Allworth Press, 1999.

Curran, Steve. *Motion Graphics: Graphic Design for Broadcast and Film*. Rockport, Mass.: Rockport Publishers, 2000.

Foote, Cameron S. *The Business Side of Creativity: The Complete Guide for Running a Graphic Design or Communications Business*. New York: W.W. Norton & Company, 2002.

Galitz, Wilbert O. *The Essential Guide to User Interface Design*. 2nd ed. Hoboken, N.J.: John Wiley & Sons, 2002.

Gordon, Barbara, and Elliott Gordon. *How to Sell Your Photographs and Illustrations*. New York: Allworth Press, 1990.

Grant, Daniel. *The Business of Being an Artist*. 3rd ed. New York: Allworth Press, 2000.

Graphic Artists Guild Handbook: Pricing & Ethical Guidelines. 10th ed. New York: The Guild, Cincinnati: North Light Books, 2001.

Heller, Steven. *The Education of a Design Entrepreneur*. New York: Allworth Press, 2002.

Heller, Steven, and Teresa Fernandez. *Becoming a Graphic Designer*. 2nd ed. Hoboken, N.J.: John Wiley & Sons, 2002.

Hollis, Richard. *Graphic Design: A Concise History*. 2nd ed. New York, London: Thames and Hudson, 2002.

Horton, Tony. *The Power of Visual Presentation: Retail Stores/ Kiosks/Exhibits/Environmental Design*. Visual Reference Publications, Inc., 2001.

Johnson, Sammye, and Patricia Prijatel. *The Magazine from Cover to Cover: Inside a Dynamic Industry*. Lincolnwood, IL: NTC/Contemporary Books, 1999.

Kovarik, William. *Web Design for the Mass Media*. Addison-Wesley Publishing Co., 2001.

Literary Market Place 2003. New Providence, N.J.: R.R. Bowker, 2002. (Annual)

Mitton, Maureen. *Interior Design Visual Presentation: A Guide to Graphics, Models and Presentation Techniques*. Hoboken, N.J.: John Wiley & Sons, 1999.

National Association of Schools of Art and Design. *National Association of Schools of Art and Design Directory 2003*. (Annual)

Niederst, Jennifer. *Learning Web Design: A Beginner's Guide to HTML, Graphics and Beyond*. O'Reilly and Associates, 2001.
———. *Web Design in a Nutshell*. 2d ed. O'Reilly and Associates, 2001.

The Official Museum Directory 2003. New York: The American Association of Museums. (Annual)

Pederson, Roger. *Game Design: Foundations*. Plano, Tex.: Republic of Texas Press, 2003.

Pocock, Lynn, and Judson Rosebush. *The Computer Animator's Technical Handbook*. Orlando: Morgan Kaufman, 2002.

Poehner, Donna. *2003 Photographers Market: 2,000 Places to Sell Your Photography*. Cincinnati: Writer's Digest Books, 2002.

Rand, Paul. *Paul Rand: A Designer's Art*. New Haven, Conn.: Yale University Press, 2000.

Rogondino, Michael. *Process Color Manual: 24,000 CMYK Combinations for Design, Prepress and Printing.* San Francisco: Chronicle Books, 2000.

RSVP02: The Directory of Illustration and Design. RSVP, 2002. (Annual)

Sparkman, Don. *Selling Graphic Design.* 2nd ed. New York: Allworth Press, 1999.

Standard Directory of Advertising Agencies. Skokie, Ill.: National Register Publishing Co., 2003.

Walton, Roger. *Designer's Self Promotion: How Designers and Design Companies Attract Attention to Themselves.* New York: Hearst Books, 2002.

Weinman, Lynda. *Designing Web Graphics.* 4th ed. New York: New Riders Publishing, 2002.

Wheeler, Alina. *Designing Brand Identity: A Complete Guide to Creating, Building and Maintaining Strong Brands.* Hoboken, N.J.: John Wiley & Sons, 2003.

Zeldman, Jeffery. *Taking Your Talent to the Web: Making the Transition from Graphic Design to Web Design.* New York: New Riders Publishing, 2001.